Training the Disaster Search Dog

Shirle

Wenatchee, Washington U.S.A.

Training the Disaster Search Dog
Shirley M. Hammond

Dogwise Publishing
A Division of Direct Book Service, Inc.
PO Box 2778
701B Poplar
Wenatchee, Washington 98807
1-509-663-9115, 1-800-776-2665
website: www.dogwisepublishing.com
email: info@dogwisepublshing.com

Graphic Design: Shane Beers — Cincinnati, Ohio
Indexing: Elaine Melnick, Our Index Lady
Photos by Lynne Engelbert, Shirley and David Hammond, and Bev Peabody

Limits of Liability and Disclaimer of Warranty:
The author and publisher shall not be liable in the event of incidental or consequential damages in connection with, or arising out of, the furnishing, performance, or use of the instructions and suggestions contained in this book.

Hammond, Shirley M. I.
  Training the disaster search dog / by Shirley M.I. Hammond.
    p. cm.
  ISBN-13: 978-1-929242-19-1
  ISBN-10: 1-929242-19-0
  1. Search dogs--Training. 2. Disasters. I. Title.
  SF428.73.H36 2005
  636.7'0886--dc22

                                                             2005010001

ISBN 1-929242-19-0

Printed in the U.S.A.

Dedication

*To my Mother and Father, who taught me that if and when I decided
to do something it would be possible, and to my husband who encouraged
me through the whole process.*

ACKNOWLEDGEMENTS

Very few authors write a book without the help of many people. I am a dog trainer, not an author. I have written many training papers, but that is not the same as writing a book. I have a long list of folks to thank for nagging me when I put off writing, and motivating me when I was discouraged. I hesitate to list them all, as I'm afraid I might miss someone!

My husband David has been a great supporter. He has encouraged me when I wanted to throw in the towel, and tolerated my presence at the computer during meal times or when chores were neglected. Without his support, the project would not have been completed. I also especially want to thank my friend James LeValley for his support and encouragement to combine into book form all of the papers that I have written over the years. Jim also guided me in some of the technical aspects of putting this book together, since I had no knowledge of how to even begin.

I'm very grateful to my teammates and associations who have tolerated me changing various training techniques and for being receptive to new ideas presented at our local trainings. These special folks include: Annie Desmon, a Canine Search Specialist with California Task Force 7—we would hash over different techniques and how best to implement the training. Lynne Englebert, a Canine Search Specialist handler with California Task Force 3, who spent hours proofreading pages again and again. Her notes in the margin would read, "I know what you want to say, but you need to rewrite this so it is clearer. The reader can't read your mind!" Christy Bergeon for nagging me to finish this book and for her help in finding a publisher. My neighbors Jean White and Barbara Ogden who proofread many of the papers that I have written over the years. And to my students, thank you for sharing your experiences and inspirational words encouraging me to complete this project. Thanks also to Larry and Charlene Woodward at Dogwise Publishing who helped reorganize the manuscript to make it more user-friendly and for offering needed encouragement. Finally, thanks to my friend Shannon Kiley, who restructured my technical thoughts without changing the content of the training program.

One problem that I have discovered in writing a book is that it is never done; it is always a work in progress. Thank you, one and all.

PREFACE

The idea for this book was conceived after many years of training Disaster Search Dogs and utilizes my personal experiences in responding to the Mexico City earthquake in 1985, the Loma Prieta earthquake in 1989, the Oklahoma City bombing of the Murrah Building in 1995, and the World Trade Center terrorist attack of September 11, 2001. There is a real need for more detailed information on the subject of training Disaster Search Dogs. While some books do provide those interested in this subject with general information, all have been lacking in some important details. Because of this, I have been sending requested material to handlers for years on how to train a specific skill for disaster searching. This book incorporates the training papers that I have written over the years into a single reference source.

The material presented will give you guidelines on how to select, train, and prepare a dog for testing and eventual deployment as a Disaster Search Dog either as part of the National Urban Search and Rescue System or as a local volunteer. There is no single recipe for training a dog. Dogs are all different and a good trainer needs to be able to reach into his bag of tricks and come up with a method that will work for a specific dog. The methods described are the ones that I use and teach in my Disaster Search Dog training classes.

For the handler who is aspiring to train a Disaster Search Dog and/or become a certified Federal Emergency Mangement Agency (FEMA) Task Force member, here is a roadmap to reach that goal. Those handlers who want to train their dogs for disaster search but are not interested in joining a Task Force will be able to provide their communities with a well-trained team to assist in the detection of people trapped or buried in a structure. Regardless of your ultimate goals, the training plan is much the same and can be used to prepare you and your dog for any search and rescue situation.

Unfortunately, in the years to come there will surely be more natural disasters and terrorist attacks. In such emergencies, there will be a continued need for trained disaster canine response units to help save or recover the victims of such events. Disaster Search Dogs that have undergone a complete training program are capable of searching the collapsed structures in a safe and confident manner. They work in search mode and can confidently negotiate the debris and rubble. They have proven themselves to be invaluable members of disaster rescue and recovery teams. With proper training, you and your dog can make a real difference in helping to respond to the disasters that will inevitably strike certain of our communities.

Happy training,
Shirley Hammond

TABLE OF CONTENTS

1

YOU AND YOUR DISASTER SEARCH DOG

The Disaster Search Dog (DSD) is one that is trained to search for and to detect the scent of inaccessible victims buried in rubble or partially collapsed structures. A disaster site is a dangerous, hazardous, and unstable environment for both the handler and the dog, whether the disaster is caused by Mother Nature or man. Not every dog or handler can do this work. There needs to be a special rapport between a handler and a search dog. They must be best friends, trust each other, and work as a team. The handler is responsible for the safety and care of his dog. The handler must know the individual capabilities and strengths of his dog and is charged to use it wisely. They will spend many hours training and searching together.

SELECTION CRITERIA

The ideal Disaster Search Dog must be very self-confident, energetic, and have a high hunt/prey/retrieve drive. He must be capable of independent work, be sociable, in good health, be structurally sound, and capable of ignoring the typical loud noises of a disaster site. While a variety of dogs succeed in this line of work, most are mid-sized breeds with a preferred weight from 30 to 75 pounds.

Breeds which may be suited for search work and that are recognized by the American Kennel Club (AKC) include several from the herding, sporting, and working dog groups; however, there are always exceptions and mixed breed dogs can also be very successful. While a whole book could be written discussing the pros and cons of choosing a purebred or a mixed breed as a potential search dog, the advantage of selecting a purebred dog is that the history of what that breed of dog was bred for is known. Simply put, the dog has the genes to be the dog you want.

I am often asked how to evaluate a puppy as a potential DSD. What I tell people is that although the dog you choose will be part of your family, it must be emphasized that you are not choosing a family pet. The DSD needs to be a highly driven and energetic dog, not one who is content being on the couch or remaining in the backyard. This is the type of dog that needs a job or will otherwise become very creative and perhaps destructive in either the backyard or the house. These types of dogs are not always the best choice for a family pet, but they can make great search partners.

"Hunt drive" is the most important attribute of any search or detection dog. Hunt drive can be described as the dog's persistent desire to find something. If you toss the dog's favorite toy into the weeds, will the dog hunt for the toy until it is found? That is a very simple example of hunt drive. "Prey drive" is also very important. You want a dog that will chase what it wants, a rabbit for example. This is something you can test in puppies and young dogs. I also want a dog that is a "good eater!" I always ask a breeder "What kind of eater is the dam? What kind of eater is the sire? Do they inhale food, or are they inconsistent, picky eaters?" This may seem an odd set of questions, but I have noticed over the years that there seems to be a strong correlation between a good working dog and a good eating dog. I have seen very few exceptions. The dog that is a poor eater is not a good choice to take on a mission because the dog needs good nutrition in order to withstand the rigors of a mission.

The potential DSD must be physically fit and have good stamina. The dog must be able to undergo a successful training program including many hours of agility, obedience, direction/control work given from a distance, and rubble search work. So you want to select a dog that will be agile and able to tolerate lots of physically demanding activity. Disaster agility involves skills needed to negotiate various obstacles that the dog may encounter during a disaster incident. Such training prepares the dog to work in a hazardous environment, which includes walking and climbing on concrete rubble, rebar, broken glass, hanging hazards, dust, or other building materials that result from a catastrophe.

You also want to select a dog that will not be easily stressed. Your first task is to find a dog with good, sound temperament and secondly, develop a good, sound training/socialization program so that you will have a dog that is not stressed by the work. This is particularly important because disaster work is often very stressful to the handler and frequently dogs may become concerned by their handler's stress in addition to their own. "The handler's feelings travel down the leash to the dog" is never truer than when doing DSD work. A well-trained dog will focus on his job and will not be bothered with the "what ifs" that cause butterflies in the handler's stomach.

The gender of the dog is a matter of personal preference. A lot of handlers are convinced that males make better search dogs because, theoretically, they have more drive and energy. On the other hand, females tend to range greater distances and are less distracted, especially if they have been spayed. In my opinion an operational search dog should be spayed or neutered. Raging hormones are not helpful in maintaining a focused search dog.

Puppy behavior or temperament evaluations can give very helpful information in choosing a potential search candidate since you can test for some of the selection criteria mentioned above. While such tests usually result in reliable evaluations when done by a person experienced with DSD dogs, a puppy evaluation will by no means give you an absolute guarantee that the dog will succeed. I recommend such tests at about 7 weeks of age as the puppy will be eating food by then and will have had the opportunity for a lot of play with its littermates, and more than likely will have had a correction or two by the mother. In general, you want a puppy that tests well in terms of an approach to strangers, a strong follow response, exhibits prey drive and scenting ability, and is responsive to affection. For more information on puppy and young adult dog testing see Appendix C.

While selecting the right dog is obviously very important, the potential handler needs to carefully evaluate whether he or she has the physical and mental make-up for the job required. You are putting your dog and yourself at risk and you must be able to accept this fact of life. When working an urban structure that has collapsed, handlers send their disaster dogs to search for live victims in areas that, for safety reasons, are off-limits to humans. Secondary collapses do happen and both you and the dog may become victims. Although this is a subject many handlers avoid, it is possible that you may face such a situation. You may also face situations that many people find horrific—dead and injured people, buildings and homes that are destroyed, and the knowledge there may be victims who may die if not rescued soon. There are so many factors to consider, but ultimately it will be the handler's decision whether to send his dog—and himself—into a disaster site. The reality of this job is that it requires deep soul-searching before you decide whether it is right for you and your dog.

OTHER TYPES OF SEARCH DOGS

As noted above, Disaster Search Dogs and their handlers must possess a fairly unique set of skills, drives and motivation. It could be that you or your dog may not be cut out for disaster work, but there are other kinds of search dog work that might be a better fit for your situation. Briefly, here are descriptions of the types of search dogs and their selection criteria.

Search and Rescue Dogs (SAR or Wilderness Search Dog)

The Search and Rescue dog, also called the area search or wilderness search dog, is used to search a specific area by covering or gridding large geographic areas, while sampling the air currents for traces of human scent. Most SAR dogs work off-lead and will range far away from the handler while quartering back and forth through the area, searching for human scent that is carried on the air currents. The handler is assigned a search area and is responsible for covering the area, documenting the area covered, and reporting back to the search base when the assignment is complete.

This dog, upon finding a human or clue-containing human scent, will demonstrate a trained alert behavior that indicates to the handler that the dog has made a find. Some area search dogs receive additional scent-specific training and search for a specific scent from an article of clothing. The SAR dog typically searches in a natural environment which may include some natural hazards, such as rushing rivers, wild animals, blackberry patches, and poison oak to mention a few. Some special agility training should be included in the overall SAR dog's training program. The dog must be able to climb and move around logjams, fallen trees, and navigate across slopes with loose, slippery rocks or large boulders along the river.

The SAR dog must be selected carefully. Not all dogs have the qualifications needed to be a success for these types of tasks. Over the past ten years, the quality of the SAR dog has greatly improved; we are now seeing dogs that are no longer handler dependent, meaning the dog is self-confident and will search out of the handler's sight. The most important qualifications for this dog to exhibit are a good hunt drive, self-confidence, good health, a sound temperament, and participation in a good training program.

SAR dogs and DSDs differ in the type of training they receive and the environments in which they must search. The area search dog receives a minimum amount of rubble and agility training and consequently, may go into self-preservation instead of a search mode when put into a rubble situation. Many of the area search dogs do not have the confidence and extra hunt drive needed to search through rubble but are still very effective working in a natural environment.

Trailing Dogs

Trailing dogs are generally used to identify a specific individual's scent apart from any other person. This dog is usually worked on-lead, requires a scent article to begin searching, will follow the trail of the selected individual, and will identify a found subject using a trained alert. While trailing dogs can be effective in SAR missions, the typical trailing dog is not an effective tool to locate victims of a disaster. A scent article is not available in the event of a disaster and there isn't a specific trail to follow.

EARLY SOCIALIZATION AND TRAINING

Potential Disaster Search Dogs must be well socialized but with a stronger focus on building the puppy-handler relationship than you might have with the average dog because of the nature of the work you expect the dog to do later in life. The puppy period is a great time for this bonding with the handler to take place. The puppy should be fed, played with, and cared for only by the handler during the initial weeks after being removed from its littermates. The puppy should be introduced to the other dogs in the house while being held in your lap. He should not be allowed to play with them at this point, but the older dogs can be allowed to smell the puppy and get acquainted on a limited basis. Later, when the puppy is older (around 12 weeks) it can be allowed to visit the other dogs for short periods while under supervision. It is important to restrict contact and play time with the older dogs in the house to short sessions. The puppy should not have the run of the house or yard with the other dogs until he is 6 months to a year old. It is best to keep the puppy somewhat isolated, except for supervised play several times a day. This visiting time is ended with a tug of war game with you, the handler. The focus of the puppy should always be on you. It is very important to start shaping this focus/behavior at an early age. The puppy must know you are the most important, highest ranking member of the family from which all good things come.

Starting with a good puppy is not a guarantee that he will be a successful search dog, but proper socialization will increase your odds. You will have great influence over your puppy and both the environment in which the puppy is raised and the socialization process to which the puppy is exposed will contribute significantly to the overall result. Puppies are like little sponges; they soak up all the experiences you can provide. It is important to provide a rich environment for the puppy. In a playful, non-threatening way, I try to expose the puppy to all of the skills, sounds, and smells that he/she will need or encounter as an adult working dog. To start obedience, I use food to bait the dog into a sit, down, come, and heeling or staying close—all done in a play mode. If you are familiar with and are a Clicker convert, great—puppies love the clicker game. All of these exercises must be positive, given as an introduction to what will follow.

When the dog is old enough, you will formally teach and polish the skills building upon the foundation learned in puppyhood.

Agility training is a great thing to do with puppies. They should have their own play area. Very young puppies have lots of fun playing with cardboard tunnels or in a cardboard maze. They like to climb on things, such as ramps and small stairs, and play "King of the Hill". All of these things should be safe and wide enough for the puppy to negotiate, measuring at least 12 inches in width. Familiarize the puppy with uneven terrain by spreading a plastic sheet on the ground with plastic bottles and small pieces of wood underneath, making it bumpy and interesting for the puppy to run across. Try placing a section of an exercise pen or mesh wire flat on the ground for the puppy to navigate. A plywood square 24" x 24" nailed to a small pedestal 4" x 4" x 4" makes a neat tip board. It will tip, just a little, and the puppy will soon enjoy running over it. All of these items help the puppy develop coordination and build confidence. Let your imagination run wild to help create a useful and educational play yard for your puppy.

Start taking your puppy for short rides to get him used to the motion of a car. Begin with a short trip around the block. Watch the puppy for signs of motion sickness. Increase the distance of these trips slowly to help the puppy avoid becoming ill. We want this to be a happy experience.

The puppy's adventures are just beginning. As soon as the puppy is well protected by immunizations, it is time to visit the world. Shopping centers or malls are great places for the puppy to meet all sorts, sizes, shapes, and ages of humans. Some will not be able to resist petting the puppy. Be sure to protect the puppy and do not let him become overwhelmed. There are many places to visit, such as train stations, bus stations, schoolyards and nursery schools, baseball games, etc. An animal farm is a great place to find chickens, ducks, sheep, cows, and horses. The puppy must have a positive experience with animals. However, do not try to do too much at one time.

Handler bonding, a good socialization process, introduction to agility, and exposure to new things are all a very important part of the total training program of the DSD. Assuming you have chosen a good dog and undertaken the early socialization and training techniques above, you will now be ready to start the more formal DSD training process.

HANDLER ASSESSMENT AND SKILLS

Unfortunately, there is not a formal assessment process for the suitability of the human part of the team. It is important to recognize that not every person can do this job. It involves a certain amount of stress and some danger. If you are claustrophobic, disaster search work is probably not a good choice. Many of the handlers who are involved in DSD training have an emergency response background, although there are also handlers from all walks of life. It is very important that the handler be healthy and in good physical condition.

In order to become a disaster dog handler, you must be prepared to make a large time commitment to classes, training, meetings, and eventually, deployment. If you are married or have a family, it is very important that your family members are willing to make this commitment with you because you will need family support to do this work. It is difficult for the rest of the family when a member goes on an extended mission, such as the Oklahoma City Bombing or the World Trade Center. They watch the news viewing all of the gory images on a daily basis and can become very anxious while waiting for your safe arrival home.

When you return from deployment, you may have emotional issues to deal with and these can be hard for both you and your family. It is difficult for the family to understand what you have experienced. Post Traumatic Stress is common among emergency response personnel. Some team members and their families may need to attend private counseling sessions to work through some of the issues. Unfortunately, a few folks have not been able to come to terms with these issues and their marriage has ended in divorce.

To perform search work you need to be a very stable person. Many handlers have never seen a dead body, except at a funeral perhaps. It is very hard emotionally for handlers to see blood, body fluids, body parts or whole bodies crushed in debris. The Oklahoma City Bombing was very tough for many people due to the large number of children who lost their lives, as well as the dismembered bodies that were present, solely because someone wanted to make a political statement. Each disaster incident is different and affects team members in many different ways. You must remember that your emotions travel down the leash and to the dog. Dogs perceive a handler's stress, causing them to question us and possibly losing confidence in what we are doing. If you are having a hard time dealing with some emotions or issues, it is best not to work your dog.

The handler needs to be able to pass certain courses and tests. Basic First Aid and Cardiac and Pulmonary Resuscitation (CPR) are at the top of the list, however you may also want to take the Red Cross Emergency Response Class or look into becoming an Emergency Medical Technician (EMT). The more skills you have as a handler, the more you can help your team in a time of need.

Potential Urban Search & Rescue (US&R) team members need CPR for the Professional Rescuer. This class can be obtained from the American Heart Association or the American Red Cross. Rescue Systems I, Confined Space Awareness, and Hazmat Awareness, are important classes that can be obtained by team members through Fire Departments or the US&R system. Critical Incident Stress classes are very important for the mental health of team members and are often available through a fire department or junior college. Course requirements do change from time to time—check with FEMA for the latest information.

2
TRAINING PROGRAM ELEMENTS

Training a Disaster Search Dog is a complex process and must be well balanced. The dog must receive the kinds of basic obedience training that any well-mannered dog should have as well as being taught the unique skills needed to develop a highly trained DSD. A well-thought out training program contains many elements. You have to choose a dog to train. You need to train the dog in obedience work. You must decide what kind of reward system you will use. You need to determine which training techniques will do the best job for the dog and then prioritize the training elements. And, of course, the handler must have good training techniques that follow the principles of how dogs learn.

It is imperative to build a sound foundation—what I like to call "building a training pyramid". Some of the elements must be taught in a specific order while others can be taught simultaneously. Based on the principles above, the "training pyramid" would contain the following elements:

The base layer:
- Basic Obedience Lessons
- The Alert Behavior
- Disaster Run-Aways
- Introducing the Alert Barrel
- Introducing the Remote Training Box

The next layer:
- Agility
- Direction and Control
- Beginning Search Problems

The last layer:
- Introduce Multiple Victims

- Introduce distractions
- Mock Tests

The top of the pyramid:
- Certification
- Deployment

BASIC OBEDIENCE PRINCIPLES AND TECHNIQUES

All dogs—including DSDs—should receive basic obedience instruction. You want your dog to perform such skills as sit, stay, come, leave it, and off reliably on command. There are many good books and trainers that can help you with basic obedience and it is beyond the scope of this book to go into this in detail given that our focus here is on the unique skills that a DSD requires. Please refer to the Association of Pet Dog Trainers (APDT) website at www.apdt.com for a list of references. *I recommend enrolling in an obedience class.* APDT also maintains a detailed list of certified dog trainers on its website.

While I will refer you elsewhere for basic obedience, I do have some favorite principles and techniques of dog training that I believe have real relevance to training disaster search dogs. These include:

- *Dogs are "place learners." This means they generally learn more quickly in their primary area for training and may not be able to perform well elsewhere without additional training.* This is both good and bad. You may have heard someone say, "My dog does it perfectly at home". The handler is not just giving an excuse. Most likely, the dog does perform perfectly at home. The problem is that the training has not been complete. The dog has not learned to generalize the training to other locations, a key skill for a DSD. To generalize the training, the dog must be able to work or perform a behavior under different circumstances and in different locations. Once the dog is performing the behavior 95% of the time correctly in one location, it is time to begin training at a new location. In the beginning, I use a 3 to 1 ratio. Train the dog three times in the primary area and then once in a new location. This is a big change for the dog so be sure to keep the training simple. Lower the performance criteria you expect from the dog when training in a new environment so that he can be successful. Gradually increase the number of new places that you train a specific behavior.
- *Only change one variable or train one behavior at a time while the dog is learning a new set of behaviors.* For instance, your goal may be to teach the dog to sit and stay while the handler walks 10 yards away. This adds up to

three individual behaviors and each individual behavior can be separated into many small steps. Each of these behaviors needs to be trained separately and then chained (put together) one at a time. First, teach the dog to sit. Next, teach the dog to stay in the position with the handler in front of the dog. And finally, have the dog sit/stay while the handler gradually increases the distance between himself and the dog until he reaches the 10-yard goal. Learning the behaviors separately and then chaining them in a sequence is how dogs learn complex behaviors best. The more that is understood about how the dog learns, the better trainers are able to effectively teach their dogs.

• *When you change or add variables you need to lower the criteria for the trained behavior.* Changing locations is a big variable for the beginning dog. Anticipate that the dog will not work as well in the new location. This means that you must make the problem very simple and gradually make it more complex.

THE ROLE OF CLICKER TRAINING AND OPERANT CONDITIONING

While training working dogs like Disaster Search Dogs have not historically involved the use of modern positive techniques, I recommend that trainers become familiar with the operant conditioning techniques as taught by proponents like Karen Pryor and others. I have found these methods make for a more successful training experience and there are a number of clicker training references, including videos, recommended on the APDT website.

Clicker training involves a set of scientific principles describing the development of behavior in which the animal "operates" on the environment, instead of the other way around. Karen Pryor states in her book *Clicker Training for Dogs* that clicker training is the dog trainer's slang for operant conditioning. The "click" is used to mark the exact behavior you want the dog to exhibit at precisely the time the behavior occurs. This is always followed by some type of positive reinforcement in the form of a treat, praise or access to a toy. It is like taking a picture; what you see is what you get. Clicker training is a powerful tool for teaching new behaviors. Some handlers may choose to use another sound instead of a clicker, but keep in mind that the timing of the click or word is the most important element in your training and most experts agree timing is better with the clicker.

Clicker training methods can be used for obedience, agility, and it is a great tool for training direction and control. If you plan to use the clicker, the dog must be introduced to the clicker before you can begin training the disaster skills. Start the training in your house or kitchen by simply clicking the clicker and immediately giving the dog a tiny, moist treat. Do not use dry cookies for this training. The chewing and swallowing detracts from the focus of the training. Continue pairing food with the click for three minutes and then put it away. Wait a few minutes and when the dog is not looking, click; the dog should come running to get a treat. If the dog doesn't come for the treat, repeat the three minute training session again and then wait as before to test whether the dog has made the connection. What you have just taught your dog is that the click means a reward/food has been earned. You can use this tool to perfect obedience skills, i.e., come, sit, watch me, touch, turn, down, stay close, as well as parlor games like play dead.

DISASTER SEARCH TRAINING ELEMENTS

Once a solid foundation of basic obedience is achieved, our focus will move to the following training elements:

- The Bark Alert - an audible trained behavior.
- Agility - to negotiate the rubble confidently and safely.
- Direction and Control - to take direction from the handler, both verbal and hand signals.
- Search, Find, and Alert on exposed or buried victims in the rubble within the handler's sight.
- Search, Find, and Alert on exposed or buried victims out of the handler's sight.

I recommend working on one element at a time while training. For example, work on agility and then direction and control in the morning. End your sessions with bark alert training. In the afternoons, move to a rubble field and work finding "victims" in the rubble. There are many options that can fit your personal schedule, but the important point is to follow a plan and be as consistent as possible. A training plan that takes small steps many times a week will get you to the desired end result more successfully that if you become very intense in your training program. The secret is to always quit when the dog is having success. Don't get caught in that "I'll just try one more time" syndrome. We will now turn to each of these specific skills in the following chapters.

3

TRAIN THE ALERT BEHAVIOR

THE BARK ALERT

The first behavior you want to teach is the "speak" or "bark" in response to the proper cue. This is critically important because the Disaster Search Dog must learn to bark when it finds a victim so that the handler or rescue team is alerted when the dog has found someone or detected human scent. This is the dog's principal job and it must be learned without fail.

The handler can begin training the dog to bark on command at an early age in his own home. We teach this is by using a reward system when the dog barks at the appropriate time. In order to accomplish this you must find a favorite toy or food that the dog will be very motivated to get. If the dog has not already identified a toy/food as his favorite, then you must go about making a specific toy/food the favorite. I recommend any type of "tug" toy. For years, many obedience instructors have urged dog owners not to play "tug of war" with their pets because it might promote aggressive behavior. Most modern trainers now think playing "tug" is not a bad idea, but in any event, remember that you are attempting to raise and train a DSD and the proper use of a tug toy is an effective way to teach the dog to bark at the right time. If food is to be the reward, it must be kept in small pieces and be tasty, soft, and moist so that can be easily eaten and of a consistency that it is easily handled. *This does not mean dry dog cookies!*

Now that you have identified a special toy or food, you can begin the training process. I will use the word toy, but for those of you who are using food, it can also mean food. This training can start in your kitchen or yard, some place that is free of distractions.

Begin by teasing the dog, then offering the toy, but snatching it away not letting the dog get it. A good way to do this is to stand in front of the dog, show or flash the toy at the dog, and then quickly hide the toy at chest level by covering and clutching the toy while pulling your shoulders forward and turning slightly away from the dog. This is called the "toy chest clutch." The handler's physical behavior evokes the prey drive and builds frustration in the dog. The dog's natural instinct is to bark when frustrated. It is OK at this stage of training to use the command "bark" or "speak" as a verbal cue along with the snatching away/teasing cue.

The handler's voice can be a great asset at this point. A high, squeaky, excited voice greatly adds to this process. Be prepared to act very silly. The verbal cue paired with the physical cue of teasing will increase the dog's frustration level. Be prepared to *instantly* reward the smallest bark with a short tug game/food and lots of praise. Repeat the verbal cue and the physical teasing cue again. The dog should learn soon to bark for the toy. Keep in mind, that it is important not to over do this type of training. Three times in a row, which I refer to as a "set" of exercises, should be sufficient for the first try. You may have to accept even less, but plan to build on each success.

The handler cues the dog to get a bark response using a toy.

Once the dog is barking solidly for the toy, increase the number of training sessions to two sets, and then progress to three sets (or nine individual exercises). Do a set of three exercises, take a short break, and then begin the next set, etc.

Don't forget to keep the game exciting and fun for the dog! When you have the dog barking consistently, begin to decrease the verbal/physical cueing. This method will work for most puppies and adult dogs. However, occasionally you will find a dog that you can only motivate with food, so you will need to use food in the same manner to elicit a bark behavior. If necessary, for some very difficult dogs, you can withhold a meal and allow the dog to earn food treats by demonstrating the bark behavior. One option that many handlers use as a last resort is to put the dog on half food rations and withhold food on training days. The dog must then earn its food by barking. *A word of caution! Any dog that is not interested in food or toy as a reward may not be a good candidate for this program. You may need to re-evaluate this dog.*

When the dog will bark instantly at the sight of the handler holding the toy without any physical or verbal cue, you can use a friend to act as the helper/victim. Now the goal is to have the dog bark at the helper in response to the same set of cues he had been receiving from the handler (toy clutch, etc.) *All of the focus is on the helper now.* The handler must stand very quietly and remain motionless. It is important that the handler not cue the dog in any way. *This is an important step in building victim loyalty,* a crucial element of disaster search training.

"Victim loyalty" is a phrase used to describe a trained behavior where the dog will focus on a particular person as the most *important supplier* of the toy or food reward that the dog desires. It does not in any way infer that the dog will become loyal to all people who hide for him. The dog learns that if he stays and barks long enough, he will get the desired toy or food reward. The dog must be convinced that all victims will be the most exciting people with whom they interact and the best source of their most coveted toy or food reward. This ideology transfers into the dog thinking, "I will stay here while I smell this human and bark until my toy or food is presented to me by the live human victim." *From this day forward, the helper will be the main focus in training.* All of the praise and play will be supplied by the helper. This is how to build victim loyalty during this stage of training.

As soon as the bark alert is solid with the helper friend, use a person the dog does not know to act as the helper. The helper must be prepared to repeat physical and verbal cueing, but chances are that it will not be necessary. Increase the number of barks required to earn the reward. Change the training location. Change the training environment again, adding distractions in the background. The goal is for the dog to bark immediately at anyone holding the toy/food in the "toy chest clutch position", without any other verbal or physical cueing.

The helper cues the dog to get a bark response using a toy.

DISASTER RUN-AWAY TRAINING

Now that you have a solid bark at the helper, you can add some new situations. Start by using a hand signal to send the dog towards the helper who should be positioned a few yards away in the "toy chest clutch position". This will not mean anything to the dog at this point, but it will be part of the patterning. You will soon be teaching direction and control, as a separate exercise, and the dog will understand the hand signal from these early drills. You can start using a search command, such as "find," "seek," or "search," to name the desired behavior. I encourage handlers to use a command that is different than any of their other commands. It should be a specific word used only for disaster searching. At this point, the dog should not need any verbal cue from the helper to display a bark alert. This is very important for the progression of the training in the future. Making noise to attract the dog's attention or attempting to verbally cue the dog by either the handler or the helper can undermine the training process. The dog must find the victim/helper and bark without receiving any cues from the handler or helper. If the dog is not consistent in offering a bark alert, it is very important to go back to review any trouble areas and then continue to progress slowly. Reviewing previous lessons in the training will help to restore the dog's confidence. The only verbalization at this point in the training should be the search command given at the start of the exercise and praise for a job well done.

The following exercises will incorporate the hand signal, search command, run-away, and the bark alert into an exciting training process. The exercises are designed to increase the dog's confidence on the rubble, strengthen the bark alert, and build "victim loyalty." Soon, you will be ready to start working on the rubble pile. This exercise uses *prey drive* to excite the dog. Think of a dog chasing the rabbit. The helper must be the rabbit, so to speak. He should be animated as he runs away. It is very important at this point that the handler releases the dog to chase the helper *before* the helper stops moving.

Helper Run-Aways

Day One, Set #1:

> The following exercises should be done in a quiet environment without distractions. The handler stands quietly and holds the dog as the helper runs a short distance and assumes the toy chest clutch position. The handler will give the hand signal and release the dog as the search command is given. This must be done *while the helper is still moving*. The dog should follow the helper and bark immediately. The helper will reward the dog immediately on the first bark. Repeat this sequence two more times.

The helper rewards the dog with a tug of war.

Day One, Set #2:

In this set, the handler will hold the dog until the helper *stops moving*. Give the hand signal and release the dog on the search command. The helper should wait for the dog to give two barks and then reward immediately. If the dog spontaneously barks as the helper runs away, that is great. However, the helper must still get the two barks after the dog reaches him before rewarding the dog. Many dogs will spontaneously bark when the helper leaves, as they know the reward will come from the helper. Repeat this sequence two more times to complete the set. The dog should now have a solid bark alert at the helper who runs away. You will need the dog to respond with the same behavior no matter what position the helper assumes. Now, you will begin to practice variations of the helper run-away

The dog should bark at the helper no matter what position the helper assumes.

Day One, Set #3:

Repeat Set #2, but in this exercise the helper will now *crouch* down.

As we move into Day Two we will start to add some new variables to the training:
- The helper lies down.
- Increase the number of barks in each exercise.
- Every once in a while, reward on one or two barks.

Day Two, Set #1:

This set is the same as the previous day's training, except that the helper will *lie* down. This can confuse some dogs and they may step on the helper. The handler must not interfere and should let the helper work with the dog. The helper may have to partially sit up during the first exercise in order to get the dog to bark and gradually work into the lying down position on following drills. If the dog is at all hesitant, the helper will reward on a few barks for the first time and then increase the number of barks with each exercise.

Day Two, Sets #2 and #3:

These sets should be a mixture of all the body positions. Increase the number of barks for one of the exercises, and then reward the dog after the first bark during another exercise. Keep the dog excited and guessing as to when the reward will appear.

ALERT BARREL TRAINING

Now that the dog is barking at the appropriate time and place, you will want to begin training alert behaviors in different environments to build a strong alert behavior. The *alert barrel* and the *remote training box* are two great training tools because they allow the helper to hide (or partially hide) from the dog. You may want to use these tools at an agility field or in your backyard to train the bark alert. See instructions for building an alert barrel and a remote training box in Appendix D.

The alert barrel is used to teach the bark alert, to motivate the slow barker to a quicker response, increase focus, and to maintain the energetic, motivated bark alert needed for a well-trained DSD. For some dogs, the alert barrel can be a terrific reward at the end of a day of agility training.

One type of alert barrel is constructed out of two metal barrels or 55-gallon drums. Cut out the bottom of one drum and weld the two barrels together. This will allow the barrel to be long enough for the helper to hide in and be fairly comfortable. Make sure to bolt cover stops inside the barrel at the open end in order to prevent the cover or door from being pushed in on top of the helper

A tight fitting cover or door must be constructed to fit snugly into the open end. The cover or door should have a handle on the inside so the helper can hang onto it. It must have several small holes at the ground level to let out the victim's scent. Some covers/doors are more elaborate, featuring a small guillotine door near the bottom through which to pass food or a toy reward to the dog. The cover should have a small window so the helper can see the dog and handler. This can be covered up for more advanced problems. The same door cover design may be used on any alert barrel, however they all need to be sized very carefully so that scent only escapes through the scent holes at the bottom. This is important in training the dog to pinpoint where the scent is the strongest. If the scent can come out in other places it makes it more difficult for the dog to pinpoint and perform a focused bark alert. It is important to consider the wind direction when placing the barrel. The barrel should be kept in the same training field, adjusted for wind conditions during the initial training of the behavior. Once the behavior is established, the barrel should be moved around to different training areas.

Another type of alert barrel can be constructed out of plastic barrels or concrete sewer pipe, and then partially buried in dirt or sand. Partially burying the plastic barrel or sewer pipe in dirt or sand helps to control where the scent can come out. The plastic barrels are lightweight and easy to move around. They must be carefully placed and braced or partially buried so that they will not roll around. The two plastic barrels are joined together (one usually slips about 1 to 2 inches inside of the other) by small bolts and then caulked with silicon insulation to prevent scent from escaping at the seam. The lightweight plastic barrel can be moved around to different areas when it is time to proof the alert before the test

In the FEMA Type II Test, one of the test elements is the "focused alert" for 30 seconds at some sort of alert barrel arrangement. In order to achieve this level of performance your first step is to introduce the dog to the alert barrel. Take the dog up to the barrel and let the dog investigate the barrel. Toss a treat or toy inside towards the back of the barrel to encourage the dog to enter. If the dog is not concerned or does not show any reservation, the training can progress.

Introducing the dog to the alert barrel.

As a next step, the helper should do a short run-away into an open barrel (no cover is used) while teasing the dog with the toy. It is very important that the dog not be given verbal cues from the handler or helper at any time during train-

The helper will do a short run-away into the open barrel with the toy or food.

ing at the alert barrel. The dog already has been taught to bark for the food or toy. Although, this is a new experience it is building on the foundation behavior the dog has learned in previous exercises. *Do not tell the dog to speak.* Wait to allow the dog to frustrate into a bark alert. If the dog does not bark, then go back to the foundation training of teaching the bark behavior.

The handler and dog should begin the next few sets of exercises approximately 15 yards from the alert barrel. The helper will tease the dog with food or a toy and then run and slide into the alert barrel. The cover is not used at this point so the barrel should be open. As soon as the helper is in place, the handler will give the dog the hand signal and verbal command to search as he releases the dog. The dog should go immediately and directly to the barrel and bark for the treat. The helper will reward the dog on the first bark and play with the dog in an excited way as he brings the dog back to the handler. The handler will take charge of the dog while the helper immediately runs back to the barrel and slides inside of it. For the best results and to maintain excitement, these exercises should be done very rapidly.

The helper will reward the dog on the first bark and then play with the dog.

Follow the schedule below during the next five to six days of training. The dog should progress very rapidly through these exercises, as the dog already knows how to do a run-away and bark alert for the reward. In order to move quickly through the process, train for three days in a row, completing three sets each day if possible. Don't forget to incorporate other types of training, such as agility, obedience, or direction and control, throughout the day as well.

The reason for the very small step-by-step schedule is that many people do not have the benefit of a training group or an experienced helper. They need this detailed guide so as not to progress too quickly. It is better to go too slow than too fast and risk missing important steps for the dog's complete comprehension of skills. Progressing too fast can cause problems that will require you and the dog to having to revert back to remedial lessons.

The dog has already done the first exercise of Set # 1 below, but it won't hurt to repeat the sequence. This time, however, the helper will now ask for 10 barks and bring the dog back to the handler. The dog must never be allowed to leave the alert barrel without being under the control of the handler or being with the helper.

Note that sometimes the directions will be given as a range of barks, such as 10-15. This is to give the helper options. If the helper feels the dog is in drive and strong in its alert, he may even ask for more barks than is indicated in the schedule.

Day One. The handler and dog will start 15 yards away from the barrel. The helper should do a run-away while teasing the dog and hide inside the barrel with the barrel cover positioned as directed for each exercise according to the sets listed below.

Set #1:
Barrel open   Helper visible   Barks 10-15 times

Set #2:
Barrel 3/4 open   Helper visible   Barks 5-10 times

Set #3:
Barrel 1/2 open   Helper visible   Barks 5-10 times

The helper has run into the barrel and closed the lid half way.

Day Two. For the first exercise of the set, the helper will tease the dog and run into the barrel. The helper will stay at the barrel and reward the dog for the next two exercises. When the helper is finished rewarding the dog, he will signal the handler to come to the barrel, put the dog on lead and take the dog back to the start. The helper will tease the dog again and then close the cover the appropriate amount for that set. The handler and dog should start 15 yards from barrel.

Set #1:
Barrel 1/2 open   Helper visible   Barks   5-10 times

Set #2:
Barrel 1/4 open   Helper partially visible   Barks   5-10 times

Set #3:
Barrel 1/8 open   Helper partially visible   Barks   5-10 times

Day Three. The handler and dog will start 15 yards away from the barrel as in previous exercises. The helper will tease the dog and close the cover the appropriate amount. In between exercises, the helper will reward the dog and the handler will return with the dog as before. In the third exercise of the set, the helper should do a run-away into the barrel and close the door. The helper will bring the dog back to the handler on the last exercise of the set.

<u>Set #1:</u>
Barrel 1/8 open	Helper partially visible	Barks 10-15 times
Barrel cracked open	Helper not visible	Barks 5-10 times
Barrel closed	Helper not visible	Barks 5-10 times

The helper runs into the barrel and closes the lid.

If a problem occurs at the closed door, the helper should start Set #2 with a run-away.

Set #2:

Barrel 1/2 open	Helper visible	Barks 10-15 times
Barrel closed	Helper not visible	Barks 10-15 times
Barrel cracked open	Helper not visible	Barks 5 times

If all went well in the previous set, the helper should start Set #3 with a run-away.

Set #3:

Barrel 1/2 open	Helper visible	Barks 15-20 times
Barrel cracked open	Helper not visible	Barks 5-10 times
Barrel closed	Helper not visible	Barks 15-20 times

Day Four. The handler should increase the distance between the start and the barrel to 20 yards. The helper will perform a run-away on the first exercises.

Set #1:
Helper performs a run-away in this set.

Barrel 1/4 open	Helper visible	Barks 15-20 times
Barrel cracked open	Helper not visible	Barks 5-10 times
Barrel closed	Helper not visible	Barks 20-25 times

Set #2:
The dog should not see the helper go into the barrel. The helper should come out to reward the dog and the handler will walk the dog back to the start between exercises.

Barrel cracked open	Helper not visible	Barks 5-10 times
Barrel 1/4 closed	Helper not visible	Barks 15-20 times
Barrel 1/8 open	Helper not visible	Barks 20-25 times

Set #3:
Helper performs a run-away in this set.

Barrel cracked open	Helper not visible	Barks 15-20 times
Barrel 1/8 open	Helper not visible	Barks 5-10 times
Barrel closed	Helper not visible	Barks 20 + times

Day Five. Increase the distance from the start to the barrel to 25 yards. No more run-aways should be performed unless needed to help motivate the dog.

Set #1:

Barrel 1/8 open	Helper not visible	Barks 10-15 times
Barrel closed	Helper not visible	Barks 30 times
Barrel cracked open	Helper not visible	Barks 10-15 times

Set #2:

The dog should not see the helper go into barrel. The helper will come out to reward the dog and the handler will walk the dog away between exercises.

Barrel 1/8 open	Helper not visible	Barks 5-10 times
Barrel closed	Helper not visible	Barks 20 times
Barrel closed	Helper not visible	Barks 30 times

Set #3:

The dog should not see the helper get into the barrel. The helper will per-form a run-away on the first exercise.

Barrel 1/8 open	Helper not visible	Barks 20 times
Barrel closed	Helper not visible	Barks 5-10 times
Barrel 1/4 closed	Helper not visible	Barks 30 times

Alert barrel training is helpful for fine-tuning, to build motivation, and as a reward at the end of a day's training. It should now become part of the dog's total training program. The progression should continue, but the training does not need to be as frequent. Many handlers use the alert barrel as a reward after doing agility or obedience training. This can be a great stress release for the dog at the end of a hard day of training.

The alert barrel lends itself very nicely to another important training goal. When the alert is solid, this is a great place to start *"distraction training."* In a disaster incident there are all kinds of distracting scents such as tempting human food, perhaps dead animals and humans, live caged animals, toys, baby diapers, and dog food. Some handlers have a problem with their dog marking where other dogs have urinated. One technique used to correct this behavior is to col-lect urine from other dogs and place the container 5 yards from the alert barrel.

The dog should be given positive reinforcement for ignoring the urine container. We need to educate the dog that during work time, it is not appropriate to snack on any kind of food, to mark the area by urinating, or to show unwanted interest in other scents that distract from the search.

CONTINUE TO FOCUS ON THE BARK ALERT

The bark alert is one of the key FEMA test elements that the dog must pass. The dog will be required to perform a focused bark at a closed alert barrel for 30 seconds. The dog must not leave the barrel and the handler may not talk to the dog until the evaluator calls time and the handler is allowed to get the dog.

   The dog's level of intensity at the alert barrel is very important to the training process, the testing process, and most importantly, to the buried victim. The bark alert is the only alert method that can be heard or recognized if the dog is out-of-sight or has penetrated a void and has found a live victim. The bark alert at the victim must be solid, that is why so much time is spent on training and proofing this skill.

   The handler will not be allowed to reward the dog with a toy or food during the FEMA test. When the 30-second time has elapsed, the handler will go to the alert barrel, put the dog on lead, and leave the test area. The dog is then rewarded outside of the test area. It is important that you practice verbal praise instead of rewarding the dog during training in preparation for the test. The handler needs to practice taking the dog away from the alert barrel *without* rewarding it. Then, the dog is immediately sent back to the barrel for another 15-20 barks and the helper will give the reward. This keeps the motivation high and should be practiced many times before taking a test. Do not start this phase of training until the dog is being prepared for the test. When the alert barrel behavior is solid, the dog should never know from whom or when the reward will be given. Whenever the reward is not coming from the helper, the handler must praise the dog for doing a good job. The handler can play with the dog after leaving the alert barrel area but this play should not be equal to the helper reward.

   With some very high drive dogs that demand the reward from the handler, giving the dog the leash or a glove to carry can facilitate getting off the test field quickly, so that the dog can be rewarded. The theory is that the leash or glove is handler equipment and not a toy; however, this may be frowned upon in a test.

The remote training box features a guillotine door that is controlled by an attached rope.

THE REMOTE TRAINING BOX

The remote training box, like the alert barrel, is a great training tool. It can be used to teach the bark alert, to motivate the slow barker to a quicker response, increase focus, and maintain an energetic, motivated bark.

The box should be built large enough for the helper to get in quickly and be reasonably comfortable. The door needs to be constructed within a frame that allows it to be raised or lowered, like a guillotine, and is controlled from a distance by a rope that is attached to the top of the door. This exercise requires a second helper to man the rope.

The door opens as if by magic when the dog performs the bark behavior. This can be a little spooky for some dogs and the dog needs to be comfortable with this before the training can progress. Some handlers find that if they go into the remote box with the door open and allow the dog to join them to get the toy or food, it results in an easier transition to when a helper begins to act as the victim. It is very important in the training process that the rope puller is positioned well off to the side, so that he is not a visual target. The person who is assigned the duty to raise or lower the rope must have very good timing and understand

Introduce the dog to the box with the door open by tossing a toy or food into the box.

the training process. Directions for building the remote box can be found in Appendix D.

Start your training by tossing the toy or food into the box, making sure the door is open and not moving, and let the dog investigate the box. Then move the dog away and let the dog observe the door being slowly raised and lowered. Take the dog up close to the door and have the door open slowly. Place the toy or food in the box and slowly close the door. Wait a few seconds and then slowly open the door and encourage the dog to get the toy or food from within the box. *The door must not move when the dog is investigating the box.* Training cannot proceed until the dog is comfortable with this procedure.

When the dog is comfortable with the remote box, proceed with the training schedule following the same plan as with the alert barrel. Since the dog has learned the alert barrel behavior already, the addition of the remote box should go quickly and smoothly. All of the reward games will come from the helper at the end of each exercise. *Watch for the change to handler rewards on Day Three in Set #3.*

Introduce the dog to the moving guillotine door by placing a toy in the box.

Day One

Set #1:

The handler and dog should start 25 yards from remote box; the helper will perform a run-away into the remote box.

Remote box open	Helper visible	Barks 10-15 times
Remote box 3/4 open	Helper visible	Barks 5-10 times
Remote box 1/2 open	Helper visible	Barks 5-10 times

Set #2:

The handler and dog should start 25 yards from remote box. In the first exercise of the set, the helper will tease the dog and run into the barrel. During the next two exercises, *the helper will stay at the box.* Once the helper is finished rewarding the dog, the handler will take the dog back to the start. The helper will tease the dog from within the remote box and the door will close the appropriate amount.

Remote box 1/2 open	Helper visible	Barks 5-10 times
Remote box 1/4 open	Helper partially visible	Barks 5-10 times
Remote box 1/8 open	Helper partially visible	Barks 5-10 times

Set #3:

The handler and dog should start 25 yards from the remote box. The helper will tease the dog from within the remote box and with the door closed to the extent shown below. The helper will reward the dog extra between exercises and the handler will take the back dog as before. In the third exercise of the set, the helper should do a run-away into the box and the door should close the appropriate amount. Once the dog has barked 5-10 times, the door will magically open and the helper will play with the dog all the way back to the handler.

Remote box 1/8 open	Helper partially visible	Barks 10-15 times
Remote box cracked open	Helper not visible	Barks 5-10 times
Remote box closed	Helper not visible	Barks 5-10 times

The dog barks at the closed door and it opens like magic.

Day Two
Set #1:
Helper in the box

Remote box 1/2 open	Helper visible	Barks 10-15 times
Remote box 1/4 open	Helper visible	Barks 15-20 times
Remote box cracked open	Helper not visible	Barks 5 times

If all went well in the above set, the helper should start the next set with a run-away. On the second exercise, the helper should be inside the remote box. For the last exercise, the helper will perform a run-away again and hide inside the remote box.

Set #2:
Helper in the box

Remote box 1/2 open	Helper visible	Barks 15-20 times
Remote box cracked open	Helper not visible	Barks 5-10 times
Remote box open	Helper visible	Barks 20-25 times

Set #3:
Helper in the box

Remote box 1/4 open	Helper visible	Barks 15-20 times
Remote box cracked open	Helper not visible	Barks 5-10 times
Remote box closed	Helper not visible	Barks 20-25 times

Day Three
No run-aways should be performed unless needed to motivate the dog. During Set #2, the dog should not see the helper go into box and the helper will come out of the box to reward dog. The handler will walk the dog away from the box between exercises and be out of sight of the box while the helper hides again.

Set #1:
Remote box 1/8 open	Helper not visible	Barks 10-15 times
Remote box closed	Helper not visible	Barks 3 times
Remote box cracked open	Helper not visible	Barks 10-15 times

<u>Set #2:</u>
The dog should not see the helper go into the box. The second and third exercise is timed for 20-30 seconds rather than a number of barks.

Remote box 1/8 open	Helper not visible	Barks 5-10 times
Remote box closed	Helper not visible	Barks 20 seconds
Remote box open	Helper visible	Barks 30 seconds

<u>Set #3:</u>
The dog should not see the helper get into the box. *The handler will go to the dog and reward the dog on the second exercise.* The last exercise of the day should end with a big paycheck from the helper!! Exercise two counts the barks; one and three are timed exercises.

Remote box 1/8 open	Helper not visible	Barks 20 seconds
Remote box closed	Helper not visible	Barks 5-10 times
Remote box 1/4 closed	Helper not visible	Barks 30 seconds

The remote box training should now become part of the dog's total training program. If possible, alternate the alert barrel with the remote training box once or twice a week during your training. For convenience, the remote box is frequently set up adjacent to the agility area.

DISTRACTION TRAINING

We start distraction training by first having the dog do a nice bark alert at a hidden victim in the alert barrel. The helper will come out and reward the dog. Without the dog seeing it, we place a distraction to the right or left of the barrel, about 10 feet away and very visible. This distraction can be a toy, not his favorite toy, but one the dog likes to play with. The dog will see the helper go into the alert barrel and close the lid with their reward toy. The air currents should be passing over the distraction. The handler will send the dog on command to find the helper.

If the dog veers off course to the distraction the handler use a verbal correction such as "Leave It." As soon as the dog is back on track and barks three times the helper will open the cover and play with the dog all the way back to the handler. Repeat the sequence. The dog should ignore the toy and bark at the helper immediately.

If the dog continues to try to get the toy, the handler has at least two options. The handler can move closer and verbally correct the dog, or someone standing nearby can correct the dog. Some handlers use a throw chain or rattle can. I do not encourage these kinds of corrections for a disaster dog and prefer using positive reinforcement when the dog does perform correctly. Ultimately they should ignore these distractions just like they should ignore any falling object on the rubble pile.

During the next training session, the handler should stand 5 yards from the alert barrel and release the dog. The dog should go directly to the alert barrel. Repeat this 3 times and if successful change to 10 yards with the toy at 5 yards. If this is successful then the handler will start the dog from the 25 yard marker. Once the dog is ignoring the toy, then add a different distraction, and then add several different ones at one time. The object is to have the dog run through all of the distractions to get to the alert barrel, bark at the helper and get rewarded. When the dog is ignoring all of the visible distractions on the ground he will be better prepared for hidden distractions on the rubble site. It is a good idea to repeat this training by frequently placing distractions near where you are working with your dog. This will keep the desired behavior in tune.

4

AGILITY TRAINING

Agility training provides the Disaster Search Dog critically important skills that he will eventually need to carefully, confidently, and successfully negotiate any type of rubble or debris that may be encountered on a mission. The dog's life may depend on how well he has learned these skills. A dog that is not confident and comfortable on the rubble will go into a self-preservation mode and will not be an effective searcher.

Many handlers inquire about whether the agility classes that are geared towards earning AKC titles are a good way to teach agility skills for the disaster dog. These classes can be very good experience as long as you convey to the instructor that your dog is a DSD in training and that you will not be pushing for speed. Use these classes to help teach the dog controlled movement while building confidence in the dog. AKC agility classes should be considered just one part of the agility training for your disaster dog. The dog still must be exposed to the types of junk agility mentioned below. Fixed agility equipment can give the dog confidence on a fixed agility course, but the dog must practice on the ever changing structure of junk agility in order to generalize the skills needed for the real life experience of a disaster.

BUILD A SOLID FOUNDATION

Before you begin training, there are some important points that need to be considered. Agility training can begin at a very early age. However, it is important to keep the obstacles simple and at a level at which a young puppy can successfully navigate. The dog or puppy should never be allowed to fall off, become stressed, or frightened by the agility obstacles. If at any time the dog or puppy appears to be getting stressed, immediately lift him off of the obstacle. Do not let him jump and don't help him continue on the obstacle. Lift him off. If possible, immediately have the puppy/dog negotiate another obstacle that he has already successfully navigated in the past. Then the dog can be rewarded and given playtime so that the training will end as a positive experience. Patience, support, and repetition are the keys to success in agility training, no matter how old the dog. Keep in mind that because agility training is fun for most dogs, many handlers often try to do too much too soon. They do not spend enough time practicing the foundation elements of agility, consequently the dog's performance will only be as good as the foundation upon which it is built.

If you are using the clicker tool for agility training, I recommend you use food as a reward. It is possible to use a toy, but the toy may end up being more of a distraction causing the dog to get too excited instead of remaining calm and focused on the task at hand. The food treat, however, is quickly eaten and usually does not distract the dog from the agility exercise. Remember, if your dog is clicker trained it does not have to have the treat immediately. The "click" marks the correct behavior and signifies to the dog that the treat is coming, but that may not occur until the end of the exercise. You may need to experiment to see what reward method works best for your dog.

The main purpose of agility training is to teach the dog the skills needed to negotiate obstacles in a safe, confident manner while trusting the handler. Agility training should always be performed with a helper. It is the helper's responsibility to prevent the dog from falling or jumping off of an obstacle. Both the handler and helper must anticipate the possibility of the dog making a mistake and need to prevent it from happening. Dogs should not be allowed to jump off of an obstacle if they become uncomfortable. Allowing a dog to jump off of an obstacle does not encourage him to trust the handler, nor does it teach the dog how to negotiate the obstacle successfully. Therefore lifting the dog off the obstacle may be necessary in stressful situations.

In disaster agility training, speed most frequently indicates a lack of confidence in the dog. The dog may rush to get through to the other side because he is not confident in navigating the obstacle at hand. Speed is most often associated with a lack of control and is a contributing factor to canine injuries during agility training. However, each dog has a natural speed at which he feels comfortable to safely negotiate an obstacle. This speed will vary within each breed, as well as individual dogs within the same breed. Fast moving dogs may need to review some of their obedience and control work to help them slow down before progressing to other agility obstacles.

Agility is a form of controlled obedience. The dog should be trained wearing a flat collar and the handler and helper should use food treats to help control and reward the dog. In the beginning, stay close to the dog to prevent injuries and mistakes when teaching a new obstacle. As the dog progresses and develops the skills needed to negotiate the obstacle, the handler should begin to distance himself from the dog. Eventually, the handler will stand at the start and the dog will navigate the complete obstacle, from sitting at the start to sitting at the end of the exercise. The handler will then heel the dog to the next exercise where the dog will sit until given the command to negotiate the next obstacle. Successfully completing each obstacle in this manner demonstrates a dog that is well trained in agility work. In FEMA testing, the handler is allowed to follow while the dog is navigating an obstacle, but must stay behind the dog's front legs. If the handler precedes the dog, they will be instructed to repeat the obstacle.

Each agility exercise should be designed to teach a specific skill. Once the basic skills have been mastered, the challenge becomes to provide as many creative variables and new experiences as possible. However, remember to train one variable at a time at one location before practicing multiple variables in new environments.

In making or choosing agility obstacles, it is important to *not make* a lot of permanently fixed obstacles. Very quickly, the dog will learn to negotiate these fixed obstacles and will not learn how to generalize these skills when new variables are presented. The dog may become frustrated when asked to negotiate an obstacle that appears similar but is in fact different, even if it involves the same basic skills as an obstacle that the dog is familiar with. A dog such as this has become programmed to negotiate fixed obstacles and has not received a wide enough variety of training in order to generalize these skills. This is an important reason why handlers are encouraged not to build permanent obstacles exclusively. It is vital that the obstacles can be moved or changed into different configurations frequently. This is why we use so much "junk" in creating obstacles.

JUNK AGILITY SKILLS

While the environment of an agility training field does not exactly replicate the rubble and debris fields in which your dog will eventually be working, it is a place where you can begin to develop the skills needed on a real mission. The use of "junk" agility allows you to be creative in designing obstacles that will teach those skills. Your "junk" should include all kinds of obstacles such as planks, 55-gallon drums, wooden spools, discarded bed springs, and rolls of discarded cyclone fencing, to name a few. Car hoods make excellent slippery surfaces and can be incorporated in many kinds of obstacles. Go to the local landfill and ask if you can have some discarded items to help train your dog. There are simple plans for most of the agility obstacles needed, plus a few creative choices, in Appendix D.

In order to negotiate the rubble safely and with confidence, there are certain skills the dog must learn and some natural instincts that the dog must overcome. Being creative and using "junk" to teach agility skills will aid in laying the foundation work needed to begin working the dog on rubble.

There are some very important factors to consider when setting up agility obstacles. The sun should not be shining directly into the dog's face and eyes. Dogs do not see in the same manner as humans and shadows can be very deceptive. Dogs can step on a shadow as if it were a solid surface and fall. Obstacles that have a grid pattern and are elevated can be very confusing to the dog. The dog may not be able to discern between the solid surface and the open spaces and may be suspicious and hesitant to negotiate the obstacle. The dog should have many opportunities to learn in a safe and controlled environment.

MOVING OBSTACLES

The dog's natural instinct is to jump off of something that starts to move. A dog must learn that he can balance or gain control of moving objects by slowing down, stopping, and lowering his center of gravity. The dog should learn to stop and calmly wait for excess motion to cease before continuing to navigate the obstacle. The see-saw and rolling bridge are a good obstacles to teach this skill. The sway bridge is a more advanced obstacle and should be taught after the dog learns to control its sense of balance.

WALK SOFTLY ON SLIPPERY SURFACES

Instinctively, dogs will use their toenails to dig into various surfaces in efforts to increase their traction. This works well on a nice grassy slope, however it does not accomplish increased traction on a slippery surface. In fact, just the opposite occurs, as the dog will begin to lose his footing. The dog must learn to relax the foot and spread his toes in order to maintain traction, keeping as much of the pad as possible in contact with a slippery surface. This is referred to as "walking softly." This training can take place on any slippery surface that you find. Begin with a level surface and slowly raise one end, making the slope steeper and steeper over a period of time. Many dogs can walk up playground slides with ease once they learn how to walk softly.

PLACING THE FEET INDEPENDENTLY

An important skill the dog must learn is how to place the rear feet in an exact place. Before dogs can walk safely on rubble or climb ladders, they must learn to "place" all four feet independently. Dogs have wonderful eye-front paw coordination, however, that is not necessarily true for the rear end. In many breeds the rear just follows the front. Small dogs, as a rule, have much better rear foot coordination than do larger breeds. This is a skill that is easier for a dog to learn at a young age and will become more natural as the dog matures.

The dog's natural instinct is to jump off of these moving obstacles.

On slippery surfaces, the dog must learn to relax the foot in order to maintain traction.

The wicket walk obstacle (see below) is a tool used to help teach foot placement and is a much friendlier obstacle to start with than a ladder. It can be used to train dogs of any age or size, and it teaches foot placement in a less stressful environment. With the wicket walk, you don't have to worry about the dog having long enough legs to reach from one rung to another or developing the rear leg strength needed to push the body up a ladder. The wicket walk can be easily adjusted for small dogs or made larger for big dogs. It is an excellent tool to teach independent foot placement before starting the dog on ladders.

FOUNDATION TRAINING

Plank Walk

The plank walk is the foundation of all agility obstacles. Although this obstacle may seem very simple, it is a foundation element that must be mastered before going on to other obstacles. The beginning plank should be wide enough (12-16 inches) so that the dog feels safe and comfortable. The dog must learn how to heel/walk on the plank, to sit, lie down, go slowly, and to turn around on the plank.

Plank Walk. The foundation elements are to heel, sit, down, go slowly and to turn around.

For young puppies, start with the plank on the ground. Older dogs should start with the plank raised to the one-foot level. In either case, have the dog walk with all four feet on the plank. Do not allow the dog to step off of the plank. Once the dog is walking effortlessly on the plank, start asking the dog to sit, lay down, go-slow and, lastly, turn around on the plank. Teach these exercises individually in the beginning and as the dog masters the skills, start to put them together in different sequences. Once the dog can accomplish these exercises with ease and confidence, begin to raise the plank a foot at a time (up to 3-4 feet). Eventually, the dog will be walking on elevated planks that may be 10-12 feet high. The dog's ability to master these foundation skills will be very important in learning future agility lessons required for navigating rubble.

Wicket Walk

Now that the dog has mastered the plank walk, it is time to introduce the wicket walk. The goal of the wicket walk is to develop the skill of independent foot placement. This is a very important skill for negotiating all kinds of rubble where the dog will find an uneven surface to move across. The wicket walk was designed by Bev and Larry Peabody to teach independent foot placement. A series of half-inch holes are drilled in the center of the 2x4 spaced 12 inches apart. The 'U' shaped wickets are made from ½ inch PVC pipe and there are an assortment of wickets from 4 inches high to 12 inches high. For more information see Appendix D.

The wicket walk teaches foot placement for dogs of all ages and sizes.

The individual wickets may be set at different heights, but eventually the dog must be able to step over the highest wicket. For very young dogs, start with the wicket walk on a solid plank that is 10-12 inches off of the ground. Set the 2x4 frame that contains the wickets on top of a plank or incorporate another 2x4 in the middle of the 2x4 frame to make it appear more solid. The first wicket should not be closer than twelve inches to the starting point. The wickets should be all different heights. As soon as the dog is comfortable stepping over the wickets, remove the plank from under the wicket walk or from the center of the frame. This will dramatically change the appearance and difficulty. In addition to stepping over the wicket, it is important for the dog to place the foot in an exact location. The dog must step over the wicket and place the foot on the 2x4 frame. Give the dog a lot of experience in this skill before raising the height of the wicket.

Start the dog with the walk approximately one to three feet off the ground, and as the dog's skill develops, raise it to four or five feet. It is a good idea to change the placement of the wickets so that the dog encounters short ones mixed with the higher ones, never in the same sequence. As a young dog grows taller, higher wickets can be added to keep the task challenging. It is important to teach the dog to step over and not on top of the wicket, placing the foot on the 2x4 frame. Clicker training works very well for this exercise. Some dogs may try to walk on one of the 2x4 rails and this should be discouraged. When the dog has mastered these skills, lower one end of the walk so that the dog has to go up a slight incline. The angle cannot be increased very much, however, as it will become steep and slippery.

As the dog is placing the foot, click with the clicker to mark the behavior. In teaching the wicket walk, many handlers use the word "place" to command the dog to place the foot. While this is a good command, it must not be over used. Using the "place" command for every movement the dog makes will cause the dog to become dependent on hearing the command and the dog will work very slowly. So be prudent when using the "place" command. It should be used only as necessary or to help slow down fast working dogs or encourage dogs that are uncomfortable in placing a foot on a new obstacle.

Ladder Skill

The goal of this exercise is for the dog to be able to climb ladders when needed and to continue developing the skill of independent foot placement. The ladder is a combination of skills involving the placement of the back feet. A dog that has completed wicket walk training can place the back feet confidently and begin learning how to climb a ladder.

It is helpful to build a special A-Frame flat rung ladder that is approximately 4 feet tall. The ladder should have a wide angle, but not as steep as 45 degrees. See the Appendix D for more details.

At this point, if the dog has already learned to place its feet on the wicket walk, most dogs will learn to negotiate the ladder very quickly. Using the clicker to mark the placement of a foot on each rung can be very helpful at the start of this training.

After the dog is able to consistently negotiate the 4-foot ladder easily, it is time to introduce the 6-8 foot ladder, sloped at a 45-degree angle. *Because a variable has been changed* from a wide based ladder of 4 feet to a narrow base set at a 45-degree angle, you must also lower the performance criteria expected of the dog. You want the dog to be successful, and although most dogs make this transition quickly, some may go more slowly after a change has been implemented. The slow dogs are usually the ones that are not as confident high off the ground. The height may be more of a problem than navigating the rungs of the ladder.

This A-Frame ladder has one side that is not as steep as a 45 degree angle.

If the dog is having a problem traversing higher obstacles, give him the opportunity to walk many planks set at eight, ten, and twelve feet from the ground. Climbing up the ladder is less stressful for some dogs than is the descent. To improve the dog's skill in climbing upward, place the ladder against a platform or short, solid structure. It is important that the dog can get off of the ladder onto a solid, safe platform, perhaps climbing down on a series of platforms or planks. Once the dog is climbing this setup well, go back to the 6 foot A-frame ladder and work on the descent. Make this a very controlled exercise, one step at a time (click and treat on each step), until the dog is comfortable and confident in moving downward off of the ladder.

Once the dog can confidently climb the ladder both ascending and descending, you can make the exercise more difficult by adding round rungs or metal rungs. It is quite possible that a dog will be asked to climb a round rung ladder on a real search, as most fire departments have round rung ladders. Additionally, the dog should learn how to use a horizontal ladder as a bridge. Start with a flat rung ladder a few feet off the ground, gradually raising the height of the ladder in the horizontal position. After the dog has mastered the flat rung horizontal ladder, introduce the round rung ladder in the same fashion. The clicker is a helpful tool in teaching these lessons of independent foot placement.

The dog may need to traverse a horizontal ladder as a bridge from one area to another.

Rolling Plank

The goal for this skill is to teach the dog to control the movement of an object by slowing, stopping, or lowering his center of gravity, rather than jumping off of moving objects, which is a natural instinct. Placing a plank measuring 12 inches wide, 2 inches thick, and 12 to16 feet long on top of two 55-gallon barrels/drums creates the rolling plank walk. The barrels/drums are positioned on their sides, one at each end of the plank. The plank should hang over each barrel about a foot. During the initial phase of training, the barrels need to remain stationary. Place wood or concrete blocks snuggly against each side of the barrels so that the barrels will not move. Let the dog practice navigating the *stationary* rolling plank several times. Once the dog is comfortable with this obstacle, move the wood or concrete blocks an inch or so away from the barrels to create some movement in the plank. Always test the moving plank to make sure the blocks are in the right place and that the barrels will not roll out from under the plank when the dog is mounting the obstacle. Training on the rolling plank should be done very slowly at first. As the dog's skill improves, the blocks can be moved several inches away from the barrels to allow more movement of the rolling plank.

Make sure that the barrels are blocked so that there is minimal movement.

The rolling plank obstacle can be used to review several skills that were initially trained using the plank walk. Have the dog practice walking on the rolling plank while using obedience commands to control the dog's speed and movement. Initially, the dog should be on a flat collar with a short lead for this exercise. The handler should use his free arm and hand as a barrier placed in front of the dog's chest to help slow down the dog if he does not respond to the slow command. Once the dog is confidently walking across the plank at a nice slow speed and with minimum movement, introduce the sit, down, and turn around commands while the dog is positioned in the middle of the plank. This exercise builds upon the foundation plank work mastered in the dog's earlier training.

After the dog is successfully negotiating the rolling plank walk, while confidently demonstrating commands such as sit, down, and turn with minimum movement of the plank, it is time to start adding some movement to the plank. This must be done very carefully, adding just a little movement at a time (1/2-1 inch). As the dog displays confidence in navigating the moving plank, gradually increase the amount of movement of the rolling plank.

See-Saw (Teeter Totter)

Similar to the rolling plank walk, the see-saw is a moving obstacle that is used to train the dog to control the movement of the obstacle by slowing, stopping, or lowering its center of gravity. It is used to train the dog to navigate a high, wobbly, and unstable surface. The see-saw is easy to construct by placing a plank (suggested measurements of 16 feet long and 12 inches wide) across a 55-gallon drum positioned on its side. Be sure to use chock blocks to keep the barrel from moving.

The see-saw teaches the dog how to gain control of movement by slowing or stopping.

As in training the dog to navigate the plank walk, the see-saw is also an obedience exercise. Start with the dog on lead and ask the dog to heel on the plank. Stop the dog in the middle so that the plank is balanced on the fulcrum. You may want to add a "balance" command to indicate to the dog to pause at this point. Next, command the dog to proceed forward slowly. The dog may need to lower its center of gravity as the plank rocks forward. The dog should then be able to descend, slowly, walking naturally off the plank.

During the initial training, a helper may be needed to manage the plank so that it descends slowly while also helping to restrain the dog from jumping off the plank. The surface should move slightly but not fall or trap the dog's feet. As the dog exits off the plank, the helper or handler should catch one of the ends to prevent the plank from hitting the dog.

The ability to negotiate unsteady, wobbly rubble is a required skill.

Dark Tunnel With a Right Angle Turn

DSDs may be required to penetrate voids to locate a victim. In order to prepare for this skill, the dog must learn to enter and negotiate dark tunnels or passageways that may contain turns where for a distance the dog cannot see any light.

First, the dog should learn to go through a simple tunnel, then a tunnel with turns, and finally, a dark tunnel. As the dog's skill increases, make the tunnels more realistic by placing concrete chunks and wood debris inside the tunnel, creating a more cramped environment for the dog to navigate.

The dog may encounter dark passageways that are filled with debris.

Creating or acquiring tunnels or tunnel material can be a challenge. Road culverts that are 24-36 inches in diameter can be used. A tunnel does not need to be round and can be constructed from wood, concrete, plastic, metal, or a wood frame with a tarp covering. The competition type agility tunnels also work very well.

Crawl Under

Crawling is an important skill for the disaster dog. The dog may crawl naturally but also needs to respond on command. This skill is tested during a disaster dog evaluation. The dog may be required to crawl under some obstacle that is half the dog's height at the withers. This will require the dog to crawl on its belly to get through to the other side.

The dog may need to crawl to get into voids or to get under debris. There is a dog in there!

To teach the dog to crawl, place an object (such as the plank walk) at a height equal to the dog's height at the withers. Encourage the dog to move underneath the obstacle. Gradually, lower the obstacle an inch at a time and have the dog perform several repetitions of moving underneath it. Eventually, the obstacle will be low enough that the dog will have to begin to crawl on its belly to reach the other side. Put the behavior on a cue, such as "crawl." Once the dog is responding to the command, have the dog practice crawling under different types of objects at different heights and for various distances. For example, have the dog crawl the length of a 4 x 8 sheet of plywood set at 12 to 14 inches high.

Elevated Plank Walk

The goal of this exercise is to get the dog from one point to another on a plank. This obstacle will give the dog experience in walking planks that are 10 to 12 feet above the ground. The first agility obstacle the dog learned to negotiate was a plank walk that eventually was raised to a height of 3 to 4 feet. The dog learned to sit, down, go slowly, and turn on a plank. Now, the dog will learn to traverse this same type of obstacle at a more elevated height. This is very hard for some dogs, so initially, the elevated plank should be wide enough for the dog to walk easily. A plank about 12 inches wide, 2 inches thick, and about 12 feet long is a good starting point. The plank should be stable and may be started at 3 to 4 feet off the ground. Gradually, the plank should be raised to 6 to 8 feet or more above the ground. Once the dog is very comfortable with the plank being elevated at 8 feet, try using a narrower plank of 8 to 10 inches, depending on the size of the dog, but go back to at an elevated height of about 4 feet. When the dog is comfortable with this, add tires, wood, and other debris on the plank for the dog to negotiate. This builds confidence in the dog while reinforcing the ability to navigate obstacles, even at an elevated height.

Walking on Rubble

Last but not least, it is important to provide lots of opportunities to walk on all kinds of rubble. This is very important and many times neglected. Handlers forget to or procrastinate getting the very young dog on the rubble. This must be integrated early in the training program. Simply, walk with the dog on many different types of rubble. At this point, the dog is not required to search for victims in the rubble; it is just getting acclimated to traveling through various types of debris. Remember to reward and praise the dog at the end of his agility training for the day. The alert barrel can be a great reward for some dogs at the end of agility training. This is a great way to end the day while reinforcing the dog's ability to give a focused alert on a victim.

The dog needs to be comfortable in walking planks that are elevated and stable.

5

Direction and Control

The Disaster Search Dog must be capable of being directed and controlled at a distance in the event that the handler is not allowed access to or needs to avoid a hazardous area. The handler may need to issue several commands to safely direct the dog to the area that needs to be searched, referred to as the "target." Then the handler can use these basic commands for more advanced sequences. Eventually, the handler should be able to direct the dog to an area without any visual cues present.

Direction and control exercises and targets make up only the beginning of this type of training. The handler learns to communicate with the dog by giving directions and hand signals. The dog learns to respond to and generalize the hand signals and verbal commands based on the foundation training the dog has received. Once the dog has learned the patterns of directionals, the real training begins. The size and height of the target must systematically decrease until the handler can direct the dog to an area without using any visual targets.

DIRECTIONAL COMMANDS AND HAND SIGNALS

To begin training directionals, the dog must have mastered basic obedience commands such as stay, sit, down, and come before beginning the teaching of directional commands. These commands are used during the initial training of the following exercises and are essential to training directionals. Review the dog's obedience commands before proceeding with directional training.

Decide which commands you will use before you start training directionals because these commands must not conflict with any other commands that you use in basic obedience with your dog. The following commands are what I use to indicate desired behaviors when directing a dog to a specific area or target:

1. "Go out"— sends the dog in a specified direction.
2. "Hup"— dog should get up on the target.

3. "Sit"—dog should sit on the target.

4. "Over"— sends the dog in a side direction specified by a hand signal.

5. "Go Back"—dog should return to a target he has previously occupied or come back further.

6. "Come" with a "Stop" or "Wait"—dog should move towards a target and then stop and then return to starting point when called again.

The next important issue to consider is the type of hand signals you will use. They must be given so the dog can see exactly where you are directing him to go. The arm should be fully extended away from the body, keeping the hand open with the palm towards the dog. The handler should face the target towards which the dog is to be sent when giving hand signals. When indicating a diagonal direction, make sure that your body does not conceal the hand signal. There are many variations of hand signals with many different interpretations as to what they mean. Choose hand signals that will be comfortable for you to use and be consistent and clear in giving your signals. Photos in this chapter illustrate the hand signals I use. Regardless of the hand signals you decide to use, make sure that they do not conflict with any other signals that you have used in training the dog up to this point.

EFFECTIVE REWARDS FOR DIRECTIONAL TRAINING

The reward (reinforcer) used can be either food or a toy although I highly recommend food. The use of food creates a fast reward system for reinforcing a behavior and then quickly re-focuses the dog on the next training task. When using a toy, more time is expended during play. In addition, the toy must be taken away from the dog and it takes more time to re-focus the dog. A toy is better used as an occasional high point reward, given at a break in the session or at the end of the training sessions.

Food rewards should come from the handler. Baiting the targets with food to lure the behavior is not the proper way to train directionals. This will cause the targets to smell like food and encourage the dog to sniff and look for leftover treats. If you do bait the targets then you will have to take the additional time to "fade" this particular reinforcement. Therefore it is better to teach the dog that rewards are given by the handler and not the target. Once the dog has performed the behavior, run out to the dog and give the treat directly to the dog.

Initially, reward the dog on every exercise, keeping the food on a fixed reward schedule. Ultimately, the final goal will be to reward the dog on a variable schedule, so that the dog will never know when it will be rewarded. If you are using a toy reward, the play should be kept to a minimum and given on a reward schedule similar to that as for food rewards. Do not throw toys when rewarding a behavior, just give the dog the toy and keep the dog on the target. Allowing the dog to run around playing with a toy breaks the dog's focus on the task at hand.

SUGGESTED TARGET LAYOUT

The following exercises are modeled after those used in the FEMA certification tests. The testing pattern used in the FEMA test is pictured on the next page (see Diagram 1). The layout is similar to a baseball diamond, and we refer to the various targets as home base, first base, pitcher's mound, second base, and third base for orientation purposes.

For training purposes, the targets do not need to be of regulation size (36" long x 24" wide x 10"-20" high). It is recommended that you utilize wooden pallets as targets that can nest inside of one another for easy transportation to different training areas. The training field should be set up in an area that is large enough to accommodate at least two targets that are placed 25 yards apart. Later on in your training you will need to set up a course that corresponds in size with the FEMA regulations. If physically possible, having a course to practice on that corresponds with the FEMA layout for every day use is ideal.

DIRECTIONAL TRAINING—GETTING STARTED

Every exercise will begin with a voice command and a hand signal. Usually, a behavior is taught first and then named. However, in training directionals, it is recommended to begin each exercise with both cues. Clicker training can be a great way to reinforce the desired behaviors when teaching directionals.
If your dog has previous obedience training in AKC or Schutzhund "go outs," you should progress more quickly through directional training. However, while your dog may already have some foundation work in directionals, do not anticipate that the previous training will automatically transfer as you begin using the target bases.

It is extremely important that you remain upbeat and make the training fun. Do not get into a power struggle with the dog. *Give clear directions and do not allow the dog to make mistakes.* It is a far better use of time to prevent mistakes than to spend time trying to correct or modify unwanted behavior. Remember the basic rule of dog training, only change one variable at a time. That is why we use the reverse chaining technique at this point. The handler increases the distance by moving away from the target base. Therefore, only one

CANINE DIRECTABILITY
Diagram 1 - Course Layout

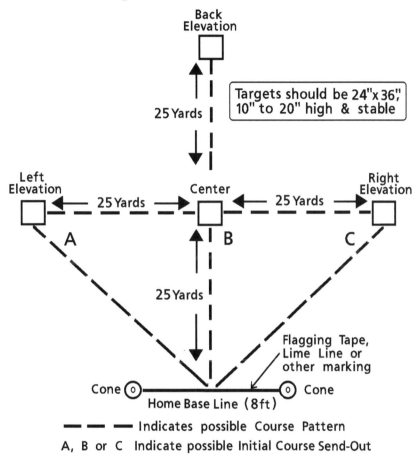

parameter, the distance has been changed. This allows us to position the target as a permanent fixture—25 yards from the center pallet in a full course. For the most effective results, train for two short sessions per day. Strive for progress, but do not expect perfection to occur in the first few training sessions. Additionally, you will be expending more energy than the dog during the first few weeks of training directionals so be sure to wear comfortable shoes.

TEACHING THE DIRECTIONAL COMMANDS

Prerequisite Commands:

Dog knows a "hup" or "get up" onto a target
Dog knows the "sit," "down," "stay," and "come"

New Commands to be Learned:
Hand signals for each of the directional commands
"Over"
"Go out" and "go back"
"Stop" and "come"

Equipment:
Targets (4) approximately 36" long x 24" wide x 10"-20" high
Leash (6 ft) and collar
Long line (30 ft)
Reward (food or toy)

TEACHING BASIC DIRECTION AND CONTROL COMMANDS

Baseline Behavior
To begin the exercise, heel the dog on a 6 foot leash to the second base target. Command the dog to "hup" and "sit". The dog should get up on the target and immediately sit. The dog must do this on command before continuing with the lessons.

Lesson One: Hup Onto Target Base
The dog should "hup" on the target and sit immediately
- Dog on 6 foot leash.
- Approach target in heel position.
- Give the "hup" command.
- Give the "sit" or "down" command.
- Reward.
- Give the "stay" command (count to 5).
- Heel dog off of the target.
- Repeat this sequence from all four sides of the target.

The dog should "hup" up onto the target and sit immediately.

Note: The target always stays in the same place. Increase the distance by backing away from the target (only change one variable at a time.) *Never let the dog leave the target without being under an obedience command* to leave the target, such as "heel" or "over." Many handlers make the mistake of allowing the dog to leave the target as soon as the dog has the reward. This can lead to a bad habit that will need to be corrected. Remember, it is better to prevent the dog from making a mistake, training only the behavior that you desire.

CANINE DIRECTABILITY
Diagram 2 -"Go-Back"

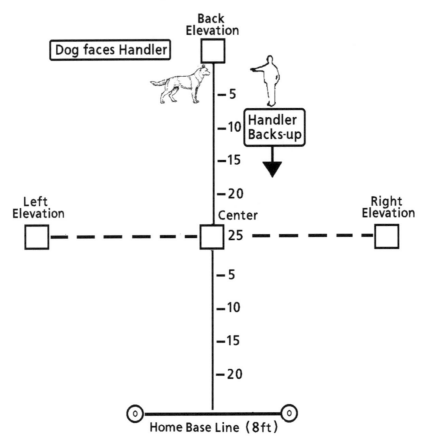

Lesson Two: "Go Back" to Second Base
- Dog on a 30 foot long line.
- Facing you, place the dog 5 yards away from the target, between second base and pitcher's mound.
- Give the "go back" command/hand signal and run with the dog to the second base target.
- Give the "hup" command.
- Give the "sit" or "down" command.
- Reward.
- Give the "stay" command (count to 5).
- Heel dog off of the target and back to the starting position with verbal praise.
- Repeat the lesson three times (one set).

The handler gives the "go back" hand signal.

Note: Marking the distance on the field (like hash marks on a football field) will help you judge your progress more accurately.

Lesson Three: Increase Distance of the "Go Back" to 10 Yards
- Dog on 30 foot long line.
- Start 10 yards from the second base target.
- Give the "go back" command/hand signal and run with the dog to the second base target.
- Give the "hup" command.
- Give the "sit" command.
- Reward.
- Give the "stay" command (count to 5).
- Heel the dog off of the target while giving verbal praise.
- Repeat the lesson three times (one set).

Lesson Four: Increase Distance of the "Go Back" to 15 yards
- Dog on long line.
- Start 15 yards away from the second base target.
- Give the "go back" command/hand signal and run part way with the dog dragging the line to the second base target. Let the dog lead you to the target.
- Give the "hup" command.
- Give the "sit" command.
- Run to dog and reward.
- Give the "stay" command (increase count to 10 seconds).
- Heel the dog off of the target while giving verbal praise.
- Repeat the lesson three times (one set).

Lesson Five: Increase Distance of the "Go Back" to 20 Yards
- Dog on long line.
- Start 20 yards away from the second base target.
- Give the "go back" command/hand signal and take a few steps with the dog. Let the dog drag the line and go to the target.
- Give the "hup" command.
- Give the "sit" command.
- Run to the dog and reward.
- Give the "stay" command (count to 10).
- Heel the dog off of the target while giving verbal praise.
- Repeat the lesson three times (one set).

Lesson Six: Increase Distance of the "Go Back" to 25 Yards
- Dog on long line.
- Add the center target 25 yards from the second base target.
- Start the dog sitting on the center target facing you.
- Give the "go back" command/hand signal and take a few steps toward the dog letting the dog drag the line to the target.
- Give the "hup" command.
- Give the "sit" command.
- Run to the dog and reward.
- Give the "stay" command (count to 10).
- Heel the dog off of the target while giving verbal praise.
- Repeat the lesson three times (one set).

Note: Many handlers continue to back up to the Home Base Line, by increasing the distance by 5 yard increments, while the dog is being directed from pitcher's mound to second base. This enables the handler to build distance between the dog and the handler. The end goal of the exercise is for the handler to stand at Home Base Line and direct the dog around the bases.

TEACHING THE "OVER" COMMAND

Place a target at first base position 25 yards from the pitcher's mound. In teaching the "over," the handler must stand facing the dog, but on a direct line between home and pitcher's mound. Teach the dog to move over to its right. See Diagram 3 below.

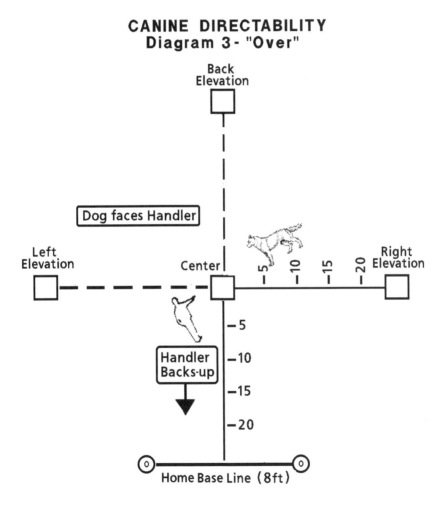

CANINE DIRECTABILITY
Diagram 3 - "Over"

Lesson One: "Over" Command From 5 Yard Distance

- Dog on long line, dragging.
- Start the dog 5 yards away from the pitchers mound/target.
- Facing the dog, the handler stands at a distance of 5 yards away from pitcher's mound.
- The dog should be on the line of travel between pitcher's mound and first base.
- The handler should be on the line of travel between pitcher's mound and home base.
- Give the "go over" command/hand signal and run toward the pitcher's mound to meet the dog.
- Give the "hup" command
- Give the "sit" command.
- Reward the dog.
- Give the "stay" command (count to 10).
- Heel the dog off of the target while giving verbal praise.
- Repeat the lesson three times (one set).

The handler gives the "over" command.

Lesson Two: "Over" Command From 10 Yard Distance

- Dog on long line, dragging.
- Start dog 10 yards away from the target.
- Handler stands 10 yards away from target facing the dog.
- Give the "go over" command/hand signal to the dog. Handler moves toward pitcher's mound to meet the dog.
- Give the "hup" command.
- Give the "sit" command.
- Handler runs to the target and rewards the dog.
- Give the "stay" command (count to 10).
- Heel the dog off of the target while giving verbal praise.
- Repeat the lesson three times (one set).

Lesson Three: "Over" Command From 15 yard Distance

- Dog on long line if necessary, change to short grab lead.
- Start dog 15 yards away from the target.
- Facing each other, the handler stands 15 yards away from pitcher's mound.
- Give the "go over" command/hand signal to dog. Take a step if you have to but handler should wait for dog to almost get to pitcher's mound before moving.
- Give the "hup" command.
- Give the "sit" command.
- Handler runs to the target and rewards the dog.
- Give the "stay" command (count to 10).
- Heel the dog off of the target while giving verbal praise.
- Repeat the lesson three times (one set).

Lesson Four: "Over" Command From 20 yard Distance

- Dog on short grab lead.
- Start 20 yards from target.
- Facing the dog, the handler stands at a distance of 20 yards away. Give the "go over" command/hand signal to the dog. Handler stands still.
- Give the "hup" command.
- Give the "sit" command.
- Handler runs to the target and rewards the dog.
- Give the "stay" command (count to 10).
- Heel the dog off of the target while giving verbal praise.
- Repeat the lesson three times (one set).

Lesson Five: "Over" Command From One Target to Another
- Dog on short grab lead.
- Place the first base target 25 yards to the right of pitcher's mound target.
- Start the dog on the first base target, furthest to the handler's right.
- Handler faces the dog at home base.
- Give the "go over" command/hand signal to the dog. Handler stands still.
- Give the "hup" command.
- Give the "sit" command.
- Handler runs to the target and rewards the dog.
- Give the "stay" command (count to 10).
- Heel the dog off of the target while giving verbal praise
- Repeat the lesson three times (one set).

At this point, chain together the lesson from "go back" and "over." Start from first base and send the dog "over" to the pitcher's mound. Next, have the dog "go back" from the pitcher's mound to second base. Then, reverse the order. Handler should move up to 5 feet from pitcher's mound. Recall the dog from second base and command the dog to "stop" at the pitcher's mound. Finally, give the dog the "over" command to first base. Give a "hup" if necessary, sit and stay. Run and reward the dog. This is a good time to quit and have a great game with the dog.

TEACHING THE "GO OUT" COMMAND
This exercise will teach the dog to "go out" towards a specified target. See Diagram 4 on the opposite page.

Lesson One: "Go-Out" From a 5 Yard Distance
- Dog on grab lead.
- Start 5 yards from the right target (first base).
- Handler stands at dog's side facing the target.
- Give the "go-out" command/hand signal and send dog to first base.
- Give the "hup" command.
- Give the "sit" command.
- Run and Reward.
- Give the "stay" command (count to 10).
- Heel the dog off of the target while giving verbal praise.
- Repeat the lesson three times (one set).

CANINE DIRECTABILITY
Diagram 4 -"Go-Out"

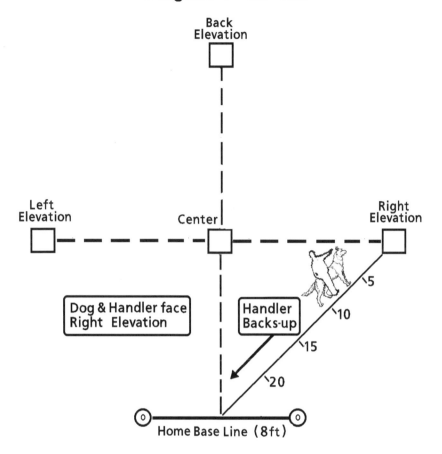

Lesson Two: "Go-Out" From a 10 yard Distance

- Dog on short grab lead.
- Start 10 yards from the right target (first base).
- Handler stands at dog's side facing the target.
- Give the "go-out" command/hand signal and send the dog to the target.
- Give the "hup" command.
- Give the "sit" command.
- Run to the dog and reward.
- Give the "stay" command (count to 10).
- Heel the dog off of the target while giving verbal praise.
- Repeat the lesson three times (one set).

Handler facing the dog after a successful go-out of ten yards.

Lesson Three: "Go-Out" From a 15 Yard Distance
- Dog on short grab lead.
- Start 15 yards from the right target (first base).
- Handler stands at dog's side facing the target.
- Give the "go-out" command/hand signal to send dog to first base.
- Give the "hup" command.
- Give the "sit" command.
- Run to the dog and reward.
- Give the "stay" command (count to 10).
- Heel the dog off of the target while giving verbal praise.
- Repeat the lesson three times (one set).

Lesson Four: "Go-Out" From a 20 yard Distance
- Dog on short grab lead.
- Start 20 yards from the right target (first base).
- Handler stands at dog's side facing the target.
- Give the "go-out" command/hand signal to send dog to the target.
- Give the "hup" command, if necessary.
- Give the "sit" command.
- Run to the dog and reward.

- Give the "stay" command (count to 10).
- Heel the dog off of the target while giving verbal praise.
- Repeat the lesson three times (one set).

Lesson Five: "Go-Out" From Home Plate

- Dog on short grab lead, if necessary.
- Start the dog on the base line to the right of home plate.
- Handler stands beside the dog facing the target (first base).
- Give the "go-out" command/hand signal to send the dog to the target.
- Give the "hup" command, if necessary.
- Give the "sit" command.
- Run to the dog and reward.
- Give the "stay" command (count to 10).
- Heel the dog off of the target while giving verbal praise.
- Repeat the lesson three times (one set).

Lesson Six: Chaining it Together

Once you've completed the above exercises, you can begin to chain them together into a more advanced sequence.

- Dog on short grab lead.
- Start at the base line to the right of home plate.
- Give the "go-out" command/hand signal and send the dog to the right target (first base).
- Give the "hup" and "sit" commands.
- Give the "stay" command (count to 5).
- Verbal praise, no treat given here.
- Handler faces the dog.
- Give the "over" command/hand signal to send dog to center target (pitcher's mound).
- Give the "hup," "sit," and "stay" commands (count to 10).
- Reward dog every other exercise.
- Give the "go back" command/hand signal to send dog to the back target (second base).
- Give the "hup," "sit," and "stay" commands (count to 10).
- No reward here, verbal praise.
- Handler moves to center target (pitcher's mound).
- Give the recall command and hand signal to center target.
- Give the "hup," "sit," and "stay" commands (count to 10).

- Reward.
- Heel the dog off of the target while giving lots of verbal praise.
- Have a play session with the dog.

DIRECTIONALS IN REVERSE

So far, the lessons for teaching the dog the "over" command directed the dog to a target located to its right. Now, simply reverse the location of the target in order to teach the dog how to move "over" to its left when commanded. Repeat the "over" lessons with the dog's direction of travel reversed to the left side. Once the dog is moving successfully to his left, repeat the lessons but have the dog "go-out" to third base from the baseline (to the left of home plate). Finally, repeat Lesson Six to chain the sequence together with the directions reversed.

Once the dog has learned both diagonal directions and right and left targets, the dog may be sent on rare occasions from the base line to the center target (pitcher's mound). However, this should not be attempted until the whole routine is rock solid. This gives the handler the option of sending the dog in three different directions: diagonally to the right (first base), straight to the center (second base), and diagonally to the left (third base). Remember, the center target (pitcher's mound) is the target that is the closest and most visible to the dog. Use it on rare occasions and never until the dog has mastered the whole course well. When the dog has learned the directional exercises, it is time to practice in many different training areas using many types of target materials. In addition, the dog should perform the exercises with all kinds of distractions.

It is very important that the dog eventually learns to take directional commands without a visible target. Sample carpet squares are an excellent tool to use. They lie flat so that the dog cannot see them until he is very close. Some handlers even cut the squares in halves, then in fourths, and so on until there is no target for the dog to see, forcing the dog to rely on the handler's directions. After the dog is able to take direction without the aid of any visual targets, you can begin training on rubble. Take the dog to a rubble pile and practice moving the dog around to different locations using directionals. Continue to give the dog lots of praise and then set up a very rewarding run-away to finish the training exercise.

6

MOVING THE ALERT TRAINING TO THE RUBBLE PILE

Once the dog has learned directionals, you can begin to work simple problems directing the dog to search and alert within a rubble pile. This is a critically important skill for you to develop with your Disaster Search Dog. As you begin to work the dog on rubble and continue training with the alert barrel and remote bark box, you will build victim loyalty while reinforcing the dog's confidence in finding exposed, partially exposed, and unexposed/concealed victims. The dog will eventually learn to search deeper into the rubble and in more complex rubble to find a victim and perform the bark alert independently and out of sight of the handler.

In the beginning, the rubble pile does not need to be extremely large. However, a larger rubble pile will give you more options in the types of problems that you are able to set up for the dog. For the following exercises, the handler's only role is to control the dog, give the hand signal(s) to direct the dog, and give the command to search at the proper time. The helper—who will be playing the part of the victim—should reward the dog and bring him back to the handler who will put the dog's collar/leash on once the problem is completed.

At the end of the training session, the handler should quietly praise the dog and take him back to his kennel. It is permissible to allow the dog to carry his tug toy back to its kennel. Take the toy away when the dog drops it or begins to chew on it. Before putting the dog away, spend some quality time with him. Examine the dog from head to toe, looking for injuries or cuts that the dog may have acquired while on the rubble pile. Then, give the dog some quiet time to rest.

EXPOSED HELPER SEQUENCE

To start your training on the rubble pile, we will focus on what I call the "exposed helper sequence." The handler should hold the dog at the starting point while the helper runs away to the edge of the rubble—15 to 20 yard—crouches down and hides with the toy in the toy-chest clutch position. The handler then gives the search command and releases the dog. In the beginning, the helper will reward the dog on the first bark with the toy/food and praise the dog while playing tug-of-war all the way back to the handler. The handler will quietly take control of the dog. Repeat the exercise two more times to complete a set of three.

The helper runs to the edge of the rubble and crouches down.

For very young dogs training on rubble for the first time, one set (three individual exercises) may be sufficient for the day. For older, more experienced, or high drive dogs, three sets (nine individual exercises) are recommended. It is important to note that three exercises per set may not be the magic number for your dog. The handler needs to decide how many repetitions are required based on his knowledge of how the dog learns best. Make adjustments to get the best performance from your dog but make sure not to skip steps or jump ahead too quickly. Most dogs should be able to perform three sets of exercises in one training day. Other dogs may perform better if they only do only two sets in one training session, but if that is the case, you should complete a third set at a later time before moving on to the next training session. When requiring the dog to perform many repetitions, you may want to give the dog a rest break between each set.

As mentioned in previous sections, make sure to only change one variable at a time. If you increase the distance, keep the other variables (such as the number of barks) at the same level. It is important to build a solid foundation. Do not skip steps or try to advance too fast. It is always best to train too slowly than too fast. Training a skill too quickly can confuse the dog and shake his confidence. If this occurs, the dog must repeat working on a skill very slowly, pushing through the point that caused the original problem. If, for any reason, you suspect that a problem is not going right, abort the exercise. Nothing is lost if you stop an exercise, but serious training problems can develop if something is going wrong and the problem is not stopped.

The schedule outlined below shows the recommended progression of training sequences set up in rubble. The distances are approximate. During each session in the beginning stages of training, the helper should use the same path into the rubble. The only variable should be to increase the distance or increase the number of barks required for the alert. The handler is to remain stationary while the dog works. Once the dog has completed the exercise, the helper will bring the dog back to the handler. Repeat each set of exercises three times. The dog should complete all three sets of exercises (nine individual problems) before moving on to the next session of exercises.

At this point in the dog's training, it is recommended that you only train on these exercises two or three times a week. On the other days, training should include agility, obedience, direction and control work, alert box/barrel training, and walking on rubble. Physical fitness training should also be incorporated, but it is very important that this is done carefully and appropriately, depending on the age of the dog (see "Canine Physical Fitness" in Appendix A). Including all of the aforementioned types of training will provide the dog with a well-balanced program.

EXPOSED HELPER TRAINING SCHEDULE

As noted above, I recommend trying to complete one session per day, a session is defined as completing each set three times. For each set, reward on one bark, then two, then continue to build the number of required barks slowly and vary the number of barks required for a reward.

Session One:

Set #1: Helper runs to the edge of the rubble, crouches down visible with the toy hidden.

Set #2: Helper runs into the rubble 5-10 yards—exposed, crouching.

Set #3: Helper goes deeper into the rubble 10-15 yards—exposed, crouching.

The helper runs into the rubble and holds the toy in the chest clutch position.

Session Two:

Set #1: Helper runs into the rubble 10-15 yards—exposed, crouching.

Set #2: Helper goes deeper into the rubble 15-20 yards—exposed, crouching.

Set #3: Helper goes deeper into the rubble 20-25 yards—exposed, crouching.

Session Three:

Set #1: Helper goes deep into the rubble 20-25 yards—exposed, crouching or laying down.

Set #2: Helper goes out of the dog's sight by hiding 20-25 yards—exposed, crouching or laying down.

Set #3: Helper goes out of the handler's sight 25-30 yards—exposed, crouching or laying down (dog cannot see the handler).

Session Four:

Set #1: Helper goes out of the dog's sight by hiding 20-25 yards—exposed (dog can see handler).

Set #2: Helper goes out of the handler's sight 20 25 yards—exposed (dog cannot see the handler as he approaches the helper).

Set #3: Helper goes out of the handler's sight 25-30 yards—exposed (dog cannot see the handler as he approaches the helper).

At the completion of Session Four, the dog should be happily moving out of the handler's sight to search for the helper who is exposed or visible within the rubble pile. The dog should be performing a repetitive bark alert and receiving the reward/play from the helper all the way back to the handler. Each exercise is designed to increase the dog's agility skills on the rubble, build confidence, solidify the bark alert, encourage the dog to use his nose to search, and to increase victim loyalty. While the dog may be starting to search for scent, he may still be relying on visual cues (sight) to find the helper as well.

7

BEGINNING SEARCH EXERCISES IN THE RUBBLE PILE

Up to this point, the wind/air current direction and location of hiding places have not been considered when setting up the training exercises. These two elements will now play an important role in teaching the dog to search with his nose. Also, we are going to increase the degree of difficulty for the dog by structuring the exercises so that the victim is no longer openly exposed. At this stage of training:

- All problems must be set up so that the wind is blowing from the helper/ victim to the dog.
- Hiding places must be constructed before the training starts.
- The dog should not be able to see the victim until he gains access to the victim.

To make a hiding place that is partially accessible to the dog, use materials such as old cut up carpet/rugs, cardboard, small sheets of plywood, or heavy black plastic. Using these kinds of non-threatening materials helps to encourage the dog to penetrate the various obstacles to gain access to the victim. Be sure to use the same materials to create false hiding places as well.

The following exercises are designed to teach the dog to search with his nose, not just his eyes. Set up the exercises so that the dog will be asked to search against the wind currents and into the scent cone. Scent tends to move in a cone shaped pattern depending on the velocity of air currents, narrow at the source of the scent and wider further away. In addition, begin to decrease the visual cues so that the dog is unable to see the final hiding place of the helper/victim.

PARTIALLY EXPOSED HELPER SEQUENCE

Carefully plan the hiding places in advance, taking the wind factor into consideration. To prime the dog for the next series of lessons, the helper will run into the rubble similar to the exposed victim exercises in the last chapter and stop short of the first prepared hiding place. The dog is allowed to watch the helper leave but cannot see where the helper hides in the rubble. The helper will crouch down near the new hiding place waiting for the dog to find him and alert. Then he will finish the exercise by rewarding the dog and returning him to the handler. Once the dog is able to complete this task, you can begin to introduce the partially exposed helper problem. In this exercise, the helper runs into the rubble and goes into a new hiding place. Working into the scent cone, the dog will use his nose to find the helper and then give his alert. The helper rewards the dog with a game of tug all the way back to the handler.

Before moving on, evaluate how well the dog performs this exercise. If the dog seems unsure of himself but finds the helper, repeat the exercise two more times using the same hiding place. If the dog was confused and unable to find the helper, the problem should be aborted. Have the helper run into the rubble 15-20 yards and disappear into a hole or hiding place that is partially covered while the dog watches. Allow the dog to work the problem as you did in previous run-away exercises. Once the dog is able to perform this exercise successfully, return to the partially exposed helper exercise again where he is unable to watch where the helper has hidden and has to rely on its nose. When the dog is confident in finding the helper by using his nose, you can begin to increase the distance 5-10 yards per exercise, using a different hiding place each time.

Whenever possible, arrange to use different helpers so that you don't train the dog to only find a few specific people. This can be a big problem for handlers who work alone without the support of other handlers or who train only using one group of people as victims.

PARTIALLY EXPOSED HELPER TRAINING SCHEDULE
Session One:

Exercise A: Helper runs upwind of the dog 15-20 yards away to a hiding place that is just short of another newly constructed hiding place. The helper is completely visible when the dog gets close to the hiding place.

Exercise B: Helper runs upwind of the dog and hides in the new hiding place just beyond the place used in the previous exercise. The helper is partially covered (1/4 covered and 3/4 open) with cardboard, old rug remnants, plywood, or heavy plastic. The dog will not be able to see the helper until he is near the hiding place.

Exercise C: Repeat Exercise B with the helper hiding in a different hiding place.

Repeat the above set of exercises in a different location.

Session Two:

Exercise A: Helper hides 25-30 yards away, out of sight, in a hiding place that is partially covered (1/2 covered and 1/2 open). Repeat this exercise three times using different hiding places.

Exercise B: Helper hides out of sight in a hiding place, partially covered (3/4 covered and 1/4 open). Repeat this exercise a total of three times using different hiding places each time.

Session Three:

Exercise A: Helper hides out-of-sight, up wind of the dog, partially covered (3/4 covered and 1/4 open). Repeat the exercise using different hiding places to complete the set.

Exercise B: Move to a new part of the rubble and repeat Exercise A of Session Three.

Session Four:

Exercise A: Repeat Exercise B from Session Three but in a new area of the rubble. The helper hides out of sight, up wind of the dog, in a different hole. The helper is almost completely concealed but should be able to get out to reward the dog.

Exercise B: Repeat the above set using another new area of the rubble.

If at any point in the training a problem develops, back up and repeat the previous set of exercises. This should help to clear up the problem. Remember that the number of repetitions recommended is just a guideline. Some dogs may progress better at a slower pace and cannot handle performing many different exercises in such a short amount of time.

BLIND SEARCH—DOG DOES NOT SEE THE HELPER HIDE

Up to this point the dog has seen the helper leave for each exercise. Now the dog must learn to respond to the handler when the search command is given, even if the helper was not seen leaving. Through experience, the dog will learn that there may be someone hiding in the rubble with his toy.

To begin this exercise, you must back up in the training process and design short search problems with the helper hiding upwind of the dog. It is important to take very small steps to avoid frustrating or confusing the dog.

Session One:

Exercise A: This should be a very short run-away into the rubble (no more than 10 to 15 yards). The helper should crouch down in the rubble to hide but is exposed. Send the dog to search with a hand signal and the verbal search command. When the dog has barked 10 to 15 times, the helper will stand up, play with/reward the dog, and bring the dog back to you.

Exercise B: The handler should take control of the dog and walk out of the rubble with the helper to an area where the dog can no longer see the rubble. The dog should not see the helper go back into the same hiding place of the last exercise. Wait until you are sure the helper is in place and then take the dog back to the same starting place as before. Now, you need to do one of two things. If your dog is excited and ready to go, then you need to stand quietly with your dog. Be very calm and give the dog a chance to air scent while he is waiting. Then, give the hand signal and search command as you release the dog. If your dog is calm and quiet, you need to use your voice to excite the dog while holding him back or restraining him. Then give the hand signal and the search command as you release the dog. The dog should go straight to the place he found the helper the last time, using the air currents to guide him. The helper will require the dog to bark about five times and then play tug and reward the dog strongly. Have the helper bring the dog back to you and together you will walk to where the dog cannot see the helper hide for the next problem.

If this technique was not successful in teaching your dog how to locate the victim, refer to the end of this section entitled "Troubleshooting the Blind Search" and follow the directions to help the dog to a successful conclusion. Otherwise, continue on with the sets of exercises outlined below.

Behind a barrier the dog and handler will not be able to see where the helper hides.

Exercise C: The helper goes to the same area as the previous problem but hides approximately five feet further into the rubble. Once the helper is hidden, take the dog to the starting point and repeat Exercise B as you did earlier. After the dog has barked five times, the helper should reward the dog while playing with it all the way back to the handler.

Session Two:

Exercise A: Move to a new location and repeat the three exercises outlined in Session One. The helper should ask for 8-10 barks before rewarding the dog. The helper continues to return the dog to the handler and together they will walk back to the barrier/area where the dog is unable to see the helper leave for the next problem. Because the helper is required to travel back and forth so many times, it may be necessary to take a break at this point and rest. If possible, try to complete all three sets for a total of nine exercises.

Exercise B: Move to a new location and repeat Exercise A, increasing the number of barks by 5 (approximately 13-15 barks). End the last exercise with a really big paycheck for the dog, making a big fuss with lots of play from the helper. Always allow the dog to carry the toy back to the car if he wants, but never insist. If the dog drops the toy on the way, just quietly pick it up and put it away.

Session Three:

Before beginning the exercises, both the helper and handler should check out the training area and the wind direction to determine how to set up the problem. The handler will need to know exactly where to start the dog and where the helper will be located. Refer to the previous exercises outlined in Session Two above and repeat this set using the same distances and number of barks. The helper should return the dog to the handler at the end of the exercise and then walk to the barrier-hiding place where the dog will not be able to see the helper leave when starting the next exercise.

For the following set of exercises, do not repeat the run-away. The handler and dog should go to a place, i.e., behind a car, building, or object, so that they are unable to see the helper hide. The helper will tease the dog with the toy/food and leave with the reward items. The handler will not allow the dog to leave the area and will wait until the helper is hidden. Meanwhile, the helper will go to a previously agreed upon hiding place in the rubble. As soon as the helper is ready, the handler will take the dog to the starting place. The handler will start the exercise by giving the hand signal directing the dog where to search and then releasing the dog when the search command is given. Once the dog finds the helper, the helper will reward the dog and bring the dog back to the handler. Together, they will walk back to the barrier-hiding place as before.

Exercise A: The helper will go 15 yards into the rubble and reward the dog on 5 barks.

Exercise B: The helper will go approximately 20 yards into the rubble and then reward the dog on 8-10 barks.

Exercise C: The helper will go approximately 30 yards into the rubble and then reward the dog on 13-15 barks.

Session Four:

For this session, move to a different location and repeat the exercises in Session Three. This will be the end of the work for the day, so remember to give the dog a big paycheck reward on the last exercise.

TROUBLESHOOTING FOR THE BLIND SEARCH

If the dog is having difficulty in finding the helper, you will need to go back and review the first set of exercises for teaching the blind search. The helper will tease the dog with food or a toy to draw him into the hiding place, let the dog bark five times, and then reward/bring the dog out of the rubble to the handler to end the problem.

Session One:

Exercise A: Set up the problem so that the helper's scent will be blowing directly towards the dog's face and nose. The helper will do a very short run-away into the rubble (no further than 10 yards). The helper should crouch down in the rubble to hide but still largely exposed. Send the dog to search with a hand signal and verbal search command. When the dog has located the helper and barked 10 to 15 times, the helper will stand up, play with/reward the dog, and then bring the dog back to the handler.

Exercise B: Go to the handler's barrier-hiding place with the helper. The helper teases the dog and without the dog watching, runs back to the *same* place in the rubble that was used in the previous exercise. The handler steps out of the barrier-hiding place, gives the dog the hand signal, and releases the dog on the search command. The scent should be blowing directly into the dog's face. The dog should go immediately into the rubble to find the helper and give the bark alert. The helper rewards the dog and plays with it all the way back to the handler. The handler takes control of the dog and walks behind the barrier with the helper to prepare for the next exercise.

Exercise C: The helper will tease the dog with the toy and run-away into the rubble, hiding in the same place as before. The handler should not allow the dog to follow or see where the helper is going. Once the helper is hidden, the handler will take the dog to the starting place and give the hand signal/command to search. The dog should dash into the rubble and bark at the helper. The helper will reward the dog on 10 barks and play with the dog all the way back to the handler.

Exercise D: Repeat Exercises A through C but change the location of the hiding place in the rubble. The helper should be exposed, then partially covered, and then exposed again for a total of three exercises.

Exercise E: Repeat Exercises A through C but change the location of the hiding place in the rubble again. The helper should increase the distance from the starting point to the hiding place. Repeat the exercise three times with the helper partially covered, then exposed, and then partially covered again.

Session Two:
Repeat all of the exercises outlined in Session One, changing the locations of the hiding places with each set.

THE INACCESSIBLE HELPER
In the next training exercises the helper will be inaccessible to the dog, that is the dog cannot physically reach the helper as would more likely be the case in an actual disaster setting. The handler will enter the rubble once the bark alert is given and uncover the helper for the dog's reward.

Session One:
In the following set of exercises, the helper will hide out-of-sight, upwind of the dog, and in the same hole as the previous exercise. While the helper will be inaccessible and *almost completely concealed*, he will still able to get out and reward the dog after the bark alert. The helper will bring the dog back to the handler.

Exercise A: The helper will come out and reward the dog as usual, bringing the dog back to the handler.

Exercise B: Repeat the exercise above, but as soon as the dog begins to bark at the *almost concealed helper,* the handler should quickly go to the area and verbally praise the dog as he uncovers the helper. The helper will reward the dog. When the reward is complete, both the handler and the helper will leave the field together after the exercise.

Exercise C: Repeat Exercise B but change the location of the hiding place.

Session Two:

Exercise A: Repeat Session One, Exercise B.

Exercise B: Repeat as above but now the helper should be *completely concealed.* The handler quickly goes to the area and verbally praises the dog as the helper is uncovered. The helper should reward the dog and then both handler and helper leave the field together.

Exercise C: Repeat as above again with the helper *completely concealed.* The handler should go to the area once the bark alert is given and praise the dog verbally as the helper is uncovered. The helper plays and rewards the dog and then both the handler and helper should leave the rubble together.

Session Three:

Exercise A: Repeat the *concealed helper* exercise in a different area of the rubble or in another rubble field. The dog must be very solid on this exercise before going on to the next step.

Exercise B: Repeat in a different area as above. The helper hides out-of-sight, upwind of the dog, and in the same hole as the last exercise. The helper should be *completely concealed* but can get out and reward the dog. Once the dog gives the bark alert, the handler goes to the area and praises the dog verbally as the helper is uncovered. The helper then plays and rewards the dog. The handler and helper leave the rubble together.

It is very important to complete at least 5-6 sessions before going on to the next step, until the dog is very sound in the blind search. It will pay off to spend a few more training sessions to build a solid foundation before moving on to more difficult scenarios.

8

ADVANCED SEARCH EXERCISES IN THE RUBBLE PILE

Having mastered the skills covered in the last chapter, it is now time to add two more elements to the rubble pile search exercises, elements that will add complexity and realism to your training. The first is to increase the number of victims. Obviously in real life disaster searches your dog will be entering rubble piles where there will likely be multiple victims. The second skill is to introduce the concept of the "handler" reward rather than the helper/victim reward we have been using so far in training. To date we have been building "victim loyalty" through the use of helper rewards, but now we must begin to teach the dog that a successful search can result in a reward from the handler.

INTRODUCING THE TWO HELPER SEARCH

Adding more helpers/victims to your training exercises will build an element of complexity to the search exercises. Because this is a more challenging search problem, it is suggested that you only do three of these exercises at a time, each in a different area of the rubble. From this point on, unless otherwise stated, each day will end with an exposed helper run-away with the helper bringing the dog back to the handler so that the training day ends successfully.

To introduce the second helper, repeat the previous problem from the last chapter with the helper hiding out-of-sight, upwind of the dog, and in the same hiding place in which the helper was found. The helper should be completely concealed but able to get out and reward the dog. At the same time, a second helper is placed upwind of the dog, 10-15 yards beyond the first helper. For some dogs, it is best to use a second helper who is known by the dog for this new step. The second helper should remain hidden until after the dog finds the first helper and the reward is complete. The handler will take the toy from the first helper and put it away for later. This is the cue for the second helper to stand up, wave a toy to attract the dog's attention, and then pop back into the hiding place. The hiding place for the second helper should be accessible to the dog. The handler will then give the dog the search command and release the dog to find the second helper. The second helper will give the dog a great big reward with lots of verbal praise and bring the dog out of the rubble with the handler following.

When the reward process is complete, this is the cue for Helper #2 to stand up and wave a toy.

End the training session with an exposed helper run-away. The helper will reward the dog all the way back to the handler. The dog should be allowed to carry the toy back to the car, take it away only if it is dropped or the dog begins to chew on it. Spend some quality time with the dog. This is a good time to again check your dog from head to toe for injuries. Then, put the dog in his crate to rest.

TROUBLESHOOTING FOR THE TWO HELPER SEARCH

If the above exercise does not go as planned, stop and rethink the situation. If the dog located the second helper *first*, simply have Helper #1 do a pop up with the toy. As soon as the dog finds Helper #1 complete the reward and all go off the pile together. Evaluate the situation. Why did the dog miss Helper #1 in this problem? Was it because the dog wanted to find a friend? Repeat the exercise using a different set of holes in the rubble and the same two helpers. If the same problem occurs, change the scenario so that the second helper is unknown to the dog or increase the distance between the two helpers by 15-20 yards. If all of these suggestions fail, have Helper #1 do a run-away into a hole that he is able to close off by himself. The handler will uncover the helper, who will reward the dog. Once the reward is completed, the second helper will stand up and show the toy to attract the dog's attention. This time, give the search command and release the dog before or just as the helper is going out-of-sight. Timing is very important for this exercise. Take advantage of the prey drive of the dog in allowing him to chase the second helper to the hiding place.

If none of these alternatives solved the dog's confusion, do a short run-away with an exposed helper and end on a positive note. Let the dog carry the toy to the car and put the dog away for the day and address the problem in the next training session.

To solve problems with the multi helper search scenario, the next training session needs to be set up before the dog is brought on to the field. There will be three helpers hidden in a row and the handler will need to know exactly where each helper is located. The helpers can be exposed or partially exposed and all three helpers will hide in a direct line in the middle of the scent cone, upwind of the dog. Helper #1 will be 10-5 yards from the starting point, Helper #2 will be in line but about 15-20 yards from Helper #1, and Helper #3 will be approximately 20 yards from Helper #2. The helpers must all be in the same scent cone. The handler brings the dog into the rubble field and gives him a hand signal and search command as he is released. The dog should go to Helper #1. If the dog stops and looks at you, repeat the search command and take a few steps in that direction. The dog must find the helper with little or no help from the handler, except for the initial search command.

Helper #1 should reward the dog on five barks and play with the dog while the handler is coming to the dog. The handler should take charge of the dog, putting the toy away for later. The handler will move a few steps away from Helper #1 and will redirect the dog to find Helper #2 with a hand signal and search command. Be patient, but firm. Use the "go out" command if you need to use it. Pairing it with the search command is best, such as "Find em! Go out!!" or whatever terms you use to start the search. The dog should find Helper #2 and bark. Helper #2 should reward on three barks. The handler will come and take charge of the dog, putting the toy away again. Repeat the procedure for Helper #3. Helper #3 will let the dog bark seven times and then play with or tease the dog all the way off of the rubble pile to give the play reward on safer ground. The handler should follow and take charge of the dog when the reward is over.

This three-helper problem may need to be repeated several times as described. Then, gradually increase the space between the helpers and stagger them closer to the edge of the scent cone. This exercise needs to be rock solid before any more advanced training can take place.

INTRODUCING THE HANDLER REWARD WITH A CONCEALED VICTIM

Up to this point in the training process, the helper has brought the dog out of the rubble, given the dog the reward, and returned the dog to the handler thereby building up a strong level of "victim loyalty" on the part of the dog. Now we are going to change this pattern for some of the exercises since, obviously, in a real disaster scene the victim will not be rewarding the dog. We will now have the handler go into the rubble to reward the dog occasionally. Our goal here is to have the handler begin to reward the dog without sacrificing the strong level of victim loyalty we have been building throughout our training to date. To accomplish this, the handler needs to be able to reward the dog just as the helper has in the past. You will keep the dog's motivation for finding the helper in high gear by putting the handler reward on a schedule of three helper rewards to each handler reward. Eventually, the dog will be put on a variable reward schedule, so that the dog will never know when or by whom the reward will be given.

To start the handler reward, set up a two-helper problem. When the dog finds the first helper, the handler will go to the dog, give lots of praise, and present the toy for a game of tug. Then the handler must hold on to the dog, put the toy away, and help focus the dog on the second helper. The second helper must do a good job of attracting the dog, with the handler releasing the dog just as the second helper disappears from sight. The second helper should be accessible to the dog, and if the dog does the second alert successfully, a great game of tug should follow all the way off the rubble. End the day's training with an exposed run-away into the rubble. The helper will again tug and play with the dog all the way back to the handler.

For the next training session, the first helper will reward the dog and then put the toy away while the second helper stands up and attracts the dog using a toy or noise. The last exercise of the day should be a helper run-away. The com-

Handler rewards the dog and helper remains hidden.

plexity of the training session can be developed slowly. The distance between the helpers can be increased, and the search time between problems can be increased.

A REVIEW OF LEARNED SKILLS

So far, you have taught your dog to perform a bark alert after locating a victim by practicing exercises using a known person, then a stranger, and then multiple victims. Your dog should have progressed from simple run-away exercises into a rubble pile to finding and alerting on victims hidden deep within the rubble and out of sight of the handler. The exercises should have resulted in a game of tug or a food reward presented by the victim, and then, on a variable schedule, by the handler.

The exercises have been designed to increase the dog's ability to use his nose to search for victims while decreasing the presence of visual cues. The search problems have gradually become more complex as the dog has been required to locate victims who are exposed, partially exposed, completely covered, and inaccessible. In addition, the handler has started to enter the rubble to uncover the victim once the dog has given his bark alert. The dog should have successfully learned how to search for more than one victim in the rubble and a schedule of three helper rewards for each one-handler reward should have been implemented.

FINE-TUNE AND PROOF

The next step is to fine-tune the search game. Once the dog is successfully searching and finding the scent cone that leads to the victim and can clear the entire rubble pile, you can begin the next phase of training. The team will need to begin traveling to other rubble piles in order to expose the dog to as many different kinds of rubble as possible including wood, concrete, slash piles, unusual environments, strange noises, and weird smells. Now is the time to ensure that the dog can handle all of these distractions.

Equally important, the handler must also be proofed and fine-tuned. Scenarios should be set up so that the handler is unaware of how many helpers are hidden. In doing this, the handler is able to practice reading and trusting the dog. Set up problems that have zero to three helpers hidden in the search areas. Whenever a negative (zero) helper problem is completed, follow it with a fun run-away so that the dog can make a successful find.

After both you and your dog are able to successfully complete search scenarios repeatedly, you should start practicing mock test searches. It is very important to set up mock tests before attempting a real certification test. Now is the time for the handler to go and observe a FEMA test if you have not done so already. This is very important, as you can see how other dogs work the rubble, how the handler reads or does not read the dog, and observe some good search techniques.

9

PREPARING FOR THE FEMA BASIC TYPE II TEST

The Federal Emergency Management Agency (FEMA) is the governmental body that oversees the testing and certification of Disaster Search Dogs. FEMA recognizes and certifies both a Type I Disaster Search Canine and a Type II Disaster Search Canine. Type II is considered the Basic Level, Type I is the Advanced Level. You must pass the Type II Test or its equivalent (see Chapter 12) in order to take the Type I test.

The next three chapters will focus on skills needed to pass the FEMA tests. Additional material you need to know in order to pass the tests is available on the FEMA web site: www.fema.gov/usr/canine.shtm. You can also find extensive information on the www.disasterdog.org web site. Both sites have lots of information and training articles as well as the Disaster Search Canine Readiness Evaluation Process. This process contains the Ground Rules, the Evaluation Process (test) and the Performance Criteria Guidelines.

Every handler should know all of the rules and regulations outlined for any test they plan to take, all of which are available on the web sites listed above. Study the Readiness Evaluation Process, the Performance Criteria Guidelines, and the Ground Rules very carefully. During a test there is no excuse for a handler to say, "I didn't understand." If something is unclear, ask for it to be repeated and clarified. If a handler does not follow the ground rules, it can mean failure. For example, make sure you do not have any food, treats, or toys on your person or in your pack. Toys and food are not allowed in the Type II Test, although a toy may be used to reward the dog during the rubble evaluation.

The Performance Criteria Guidelines are extremely important. They establish the criteria that the evaluators must adhere to in order to determine whether you will pass or fail. It will give you an overall understanding of the importance of each exercise and what the evaluators expect to see.

With that said, let's look briefly at what the team needs to do in order to pass the Basic test (more detailed information will follow):

- Obedience: the dog must demonstrate command of several obedience skills including heeling with distractions, recalls, and a long down.
- Bark alert: the dog must demonstrate a 30 second focused bark alert after finding a hidden victim in an alert barrel or tube.
- Direction and control: the handler must direct the dog to 4 or 5 targets arranged in a pattern similar to a baseball diamond. The dog must take direction to the proper target, get on the target and remain there for 5 seconds and finish the course within 3 minutes.
- Agility: the dog must complete 5 of 6 obstacles, including the mandatory ladder, elevated plank, right angle tunnel and a wobbly surface. The dog must demonstrate a slow, a stop, and a turn about on command on an obstacle and complete the course in five minutes.
- Rubble search: the dog must search the rubble independently and find and alert on two victims, demonstrating a focused bark on live human scent with no false alerts. The dog must show a focused commitment to each victim until the handler arrives and pinpoint the area of the strongest scent source.

Remember, evaluators are not your enemy. If you have a question, ask their personal opinions on what they would do in a certain situation or what their expectations would include. Most evaluators are more than happy to share their knowledge with you, with the exception of telling you where the victims are located.

In order to prepare for the FEMA Type II Basic Test, you and your dog must start putting all of the pieces together. A plan must be developed to integrate obedience, direction and control, agility, the bark alert, and rubble work together on one of your training days. Many handlers forget to practice all the elements on the *same* day. In California, the FEMA National Canine Readiness Evaluation is occasionally divided into two parts. The first four elements are given on one day and if the team passes, they are eligible to take the fifth element, the rubble test, at a different time and location. In some cases the first four elements are tested and those that pass will go on to take the rubble test on the same day. However, this whole routine—all five elements—needs to be practiced on a given day no less than a week before the test. On the rest of the days, you can still do maintenance work on the other skills and keep your dog physically in shape. See Canine Fitness in Appendix A. The handler should also practice interview skills and how to develop a search plan for the rubble search scenario that is given at the briefing.

It is very important that you continue to keep the dog motivated. Runaway searches will likely to have proven to have been the most motivating part of training for the dog and you should continue to work them into your training routines frequently. They are both fun for the dog and a very important skill for the dog to master.

TYPE II TEST OVERVIEW

The testing process is composed of five elements. The first four elements evaluate specific skills such as obedience (which includes testing for aggression toward humans or dogs), the alert behavior, direction and control, and agility. The fifth element evaluates the search and rubble skills, plus all of the other skills involved in searching the rubble. A standard course has been designed to evaluate each skill.

Element One—Obedience

The first exercise evaluates the sociability of the dog under unusual circumstances to determine whether he may be frightened by or aggressive towards humans. The handler will be asked to tie the dog to a fence or some other suitable object where the dog will be safe. The handler will not give the dog any special command, but will leave the dog and proceed to a hiding place for the duration of one minute. The evaluator will designate a person who is not familiar with the dog to untie the dog and take him to the waiting handler when the one-minute time frame has elapsed. It is amazing how many handlers never practice this exercise before the test. The dog should not show any fear or aggression towards the person that unties the dog and takes him to the handler. This skill is necessary as there may be a situation during a mission or training session where you might be hurt and someone totally unfamiliar to the dog may need to move him.

The second exercise is to determine whether the dog is aggressive toward other dogs. You will be asked to do a figure 8 pattern around two handlers with their dogs sitting beside them as posts. The testing team should be careful not to step on the tail of the post dogs, but should pass within a two foot distance of each dog. About half way through the exercise the evaluator will ask you to reverse direction. This is to assure that your dog has had an opportunity to pass face to face with each of the post dogs. Unlike an AKC exercise, you are allowed to talk to your dog and it is your job to keep the dog focused on you. Do not let your dog make eye-to-eye contact or sniff the post dogs. Do not set your dog up for failure. Another important point is to keep a loose lead. The clip to the collar should be pointing to the ground. Keeping your dog on a loose lead will help reduce any stress from occurring. If you are tense your dog may sense it and may react inappropriately!

The off lead obedience exercise will determine if the dog is obedient and responsive to the handler. It is permissible to use more than one command, however, the handler should not need to use repetitive commands. The area used to evaluate the obedience exercises needs to be large enough to perform the designated exercises, staying clear of hazards. The dog should heel off lead through a group of milling folks. The dog should pay attention to you and not sniff the random people or become distracted by them. The dog should focus on you, heel with you, and change pace as you change pace or stop. You are allowed to talk to your dog, but if you have to pat your side and talk to the dog constantly it may cause you to fail.

The next exercise, the Emergency Stop, can cause a lot of heartache for handlers. The dog seems to know you are nervous and many will not respond as usual. In this exercise, the dog will be placed at a marker 25 yards from the base line where the handler must stand. The handler is allowed to give a hand signal, a voice command, or use a whistle to call the dog and then stop him when the evaluator gives the stop signal. If there is the slightest doubt that the dog is not going to stop, be quick and give a second command. One technique, used successfully with fast-moving dogs, is for the handler to stand a good stride behind the 25-foot base line. This gives the handler the opportunity to step toward the dog with lots of body movement as you give the stop command. The dog perceives this as a more forceful command. The dog must immediately change gait when the command is given and come to a stop. The dog may sit, down, or stand in place.

The long down or wait is the next exercise. This is an important exercise and while you may never leave a dog unattended, you may need to have the dog stay in a safe place while you assist a team member. Do not underestimate the value of training beyond the required skill. The dog should be capable of staying with the handler's backpack while the handler is out of sight for five minutes. The dog may stand, sit, or change position as long as it stays within a body length of the pack and where the dog was positioned when you left. When you return to the dog, it is permissible to tell the dog to stay if needed. The exercise is not over until the evaluator states, "exercise complete." Keep the dog under control as you praise your dog and put on the leash.

Element Two—Bark Alert Behavior

In this exercise, the team has five minutes to complete the bark alert exercise. In a disaster incident, the bark alert is the alert of choice. It is the only alert method that can be recognized from out-of-sight, hazardous areas where it is unsafe for the handler to enter. The exercise is designed to test the dog's focus and ability to bark alert for 30 seconds at a concealed victim in a sterile environment, not on the rubble site. The victim will be hidden in a bark barrel or concrete tube with a snug fitting lid/door, and the barrel/tube is usually partially buried in dirt, sand, or wood chips. The lid/door will have a few holes near the ground so scent can escape. The tube is usually buried so the scent can only escape from the front in order to best evaluate the dog's focus on scent and alert behavior. See Appendix D for drawings of the bark barrel and lid.

Element Three—Direction and Control

This is a direction and control exercise in which the team has three minutes to complete the exercise. This course tests the dog's response to directionals. On a real mission, the dog must be directable in order to cover the assigned search area, to avoid hazardous areas or redirect the dog to search an area more than once. He must learn to take directions that are visual as well as audible.

For the purpose of testing this skill, the direction and control course is laid out like the baseball diamond as shown in Chapter 5. Handler technique is important and the evaluators will explain the pattern that you are to direct your dog. When you approach the course with your dog, walk to the starting line in the same direction you will be sending the dog. The dog's head and tail should line up with the target where the dog will be sent. This helps the dog focus on the correct target.

All bases/targets are elevated 10-20 inches high. All bases/targets are 25 yards from the center base/target or pitchers mound, which is 25 yards from the starting line at home base. The course layout area should be large enough to accommodate the pattern and be clear of objects that might confuse the dog and cause him to make the wrong choice. The evaluator will designate the pattern the handler must direct the dog to perform.

The handler stays at the home base line and directs the dog to the designated targets. The dog must go up onto the correct base/target and wait there for five seconds before being directed to the next base/target. The dog then is directed to four or five of these bases/targets and then recalled to the handler. Since, the dog must stay for five seconds on the target, make sure to practice at least ten seconds so that the dog performs at his best for the test. The dog may sit, stand, or down on the target. Whatever the dog normally does, do not change this on the day of the evaluation.

Element Four—Agility

For this exercise, the team will have five minutes to complete an agility course. The handlers are usually allowed to walk through the course as a group without their dogs first. It is a good idea to check obstacles to see that they are secure. If you have a concern, talk to the evaluators. Canine safety is important and the handler should always be responsible for the dog. The agility course area must be large enough for the six obstacles to be placed within it. There are 4 mandatory obstacles: an 8 foot ladder set at a 45 degree angle; an elevated plank walk 6-8 feet off of the ground; a 3 foot high wobbly, unsteady surface; and a dark narrow tunnel/passageway containing at least one right angle turn. The evaluators choose two other obstacles to make up the six required for the test. The choices for the other two may be a see-saw, a moving plank suspended on two 50-gallon drums, a slippery, unpleasant surface or an object that requires the dog to crawl on his belly. This last object must be adjusted for each dog so that the height of the object is half the dog's height at the withers.

Ideally, the handler should be able to direct the dog without moving from the starting position at each obstacle, while the dog negotiates each obstacle in a safe and controlled manner. However, the handler is permitted to follow the dog, but must stay behind the dog's shoulders. The dog must demonstrate a stop, turn, and slow behavior on the handler's command while on any obstacle. In order to pass the exercise, the dog must complete five of the six obstacles, including all four of the mandatory obstacles.

Element Five—Rubble Search

In this portion of the test, the handler and dog will have to demonstrate their ability to integrate all of the previously evaluated elements at a realistic, simulated disaster site.

The rubble site will contain 3500-5000 square feet of rubble, with an average depth of 10 feet. It will consist predominantly of concrete, or a mixture of materials commonly found at a disaster site. There will be two well-concealed victims, out of the handler's sight, within the rubble pile.

During the search for the first victim, the handler is not allowed on the rubble until the dog alerts. Then the handler may go to the alert location, praise the dog, and indicate the location of the victim. This search assesses the dog's ability to work independently from the handler to find the victim's location and perform the bark alert out of the handler's sight.

The second part of the search will evaluate how the dog and handler work together, the responsiveness of the dog to the handler's direction, the handler's search strategy, and the handler's agility on the rubble. You will be briefed by the evaluators before entering the rubble. Pay very close attention to the briefing scenario. It may seem silly or unreal but it often contains valuable clues as to where the victims may be located. This will enable you to direct the dog to search the pile efficiently.

One evaluator follows the handler on the rubble pile during the search. The other two evaluators position themselves in a convenient place on the rubble where they can observe the search work. The handler must describe to the evaluator *where the victim is located*. This is a very important part of passing the test. It is up to the handler to read the dog and determine where he is pinpointing the scent. The handler must relate this to the evaluator.

When asked, "Where is the victim located?" the handler should answer in a fashion such as: "My dog has alerted and indicates that the scent is strongest right here where I have placed this orange tape. Considering the wind direction, wind speed, and how scent channels through the debris, the rescue team should concentrate on a five-foot area around this point. I advise you to have the location checked by another search dog before the rescue team starts operations."

SETTING UP A MOCK TEST

This section discusses how to properly plan for a mock test focusing on rubble search so that the handler and dog can practice a simulated scenario to prepare for the certification test and real world situations. The rubble pile should be large enough to hide two victims, between 3500 and 5000 square feet, a minimum of 10 feet average depth, and laid out so it is searchable in 15 minutes. There should be a clearly marked area in which the handler must stay to direct the dog to search for one out-of-sight victim. Two victims should be concealed in places that are not visible to the handler from the starting area. This will ensure that the dog will have an opportunity to find and perform a bark alert on a hidden victim who is out of the handler's sight.

The handler is briefed with a planned scenario. It is important for the handler to ask appropriate questions to establish a search plan that will be efficient and safe (referred to as establishing "Scene Safety"). Follow the interview checklist outlined in Appendix E. The handler should wear all the appropriate safety gear and have on his/her person all of the other gear that may be needed. Besides

Two victims are well hidden within this rubble pile.

your interview cheat sheet, you should have a notebook and pen to write down the scenario details and other pertinent information.

The handler then commands the dog to search from a designated area and may not move from this area until the dog has alerted. Once the dog has barked at least three times, the handler may go to the dog, indicate to the evaluator where the victim is concealed, and mark the area with orange flagging tape. At this point, the handler and dog may now search anywhere on the rubble pile to find the second victim. The dog must find, bark, and indicate to the handler where the second victim is concealed.

The first part of the evaluation reviews how the dog searches and alerts on a victim who is out of the handler's sight. The second part of the evaluation assesses how the team works together. Does the handler have a reasonable search plan? Does the dog continue to search independently when out of the handler's sight? Can the handler direct the dog on the rubble as needed?

Remember to examine your dog after completing the search, whether it is a mock scenario or the real thing. This should be done before the handler debriefs, unless the evaluators direct you otherwise. Give the dog a good "tail to nose" exam, checking for any injury, scrapes, or cuts.

In the debriefing, you will be asked how many victims your dog found and the locations of each of them. You will be asked to explain your sketch map. For the Basic (Type II) Test, the handler does not need to sketch the search site and mark the location of the victims. However, it is a good idea to practice this skill, as the handler will have to draw a sketch on the Advanced (Type I) Test. This sounds simple, but most handlers have a difficult time making a useful sketch. The sketch should contain enough landmarks so that anyone could use the map to find the location of the victim.

It is advised that each handler practice the entire mock test several times before taking the real test. This will help instill confidence in the handler while preparing for the actual test. The handler should only attempt to take the test when both the dog and handler have been able to successfully complete the mock test several times and are confident in their abilities.

10
TRAINING FOR THE ADVANCED TYPE I TEST

Once you have passed the Basic (Type II) Test, it is time to prepare for the Advanced (Type I) Test. The Advanced Test focuses on what FEMA terms "disaster search operations." While the Basic Test requires the dog to bark alert on two victims with no false alerts within one rubble pile, the Advanced Test requires the search team to cover three separate search sites, locate five of six victims and have no more than one false alert. It also has more rigorous performance criteria and evaluation guidelines. Here are some training tips and exercises I recommend to get prepared for the Advanced Test.

KEEP PRACTICING BASIC SKILLS

A big mistake that many handlers make is to stop training on the fundamental elements. It is very important to continue practicing obedience and agility skills. Try new things, make known obstacles more difficult, and strive to improve the dog's coordination. Make sure you train with all kinds of distractions within the search area. Make a plan listing many distractions and unusual situations and incorporate them into your training scenarios (see below for suggestions). Advanced search dogs must be capable of searching for extended periods of time during deployment. It is important to maintain peak physical conditioning—both you and your dog—throughout your careers.

The direction and control skills that were evaluated during the Basic Test are just the tip of the iceberg. Directional control at a distance is crucial to the search and the handler must always continue training the dog on the rubble pile. The dog should reach a level of proficiency that will enable you to send the dog in any direction, at least fifty yards, without a visible target. This is a very valuable skill. For example, you look at the rubble pile and decide to send the dog to search a prominent feature. You cannot describe that prominent feature to your dog, so you must direct the dog using a series of commands. The dog is sent in the general direction and as the dog gets closer to the object, you can adjust the direction of travel. There may be a hazardous area around which the dog needs to be directed. Once the dog is clear of the hazard, you can continue directing the dog toward the target object, making any small adjustments as needed. When the dog can work at this level, the handler has a valuable search tool and is ready for deployment. Direction and control work is an ongoing training task throughout the dog's career.

The handler directing the dog on the rubble pile.

MULTIPLE VICTIMS

As noted above, the Basic (Type II) dog must be able to find, alert, and indicate the location of two victims. The Type I Test will require your dog to find, alert on, and indicate at least five victims. This is not difficult for most dogs if the training program provides for the transition. Plan a training routine by searching for two concealed victims initially and then add one exposed victim per session until you reach five total victims.

During the first exercise, the first victim will be partially exposed and the helper will reward the dog when the victim is found. The second victim should be a concealed victim with the handler opening the hiding place so that the helper can reward the dog. The third victim should be an exposed helper who will play with/reward the dog away from the rubble pile. The last reward session should feature a jackpot reward. Give the dog a 10-15 minute rest period and then repeat the exercise on a different pile. If the dog has a problem locating the third victim, have the victim pop-up and then lay down. This should help to solve the problem. If the dog is still confused, move the helper closer and check the wind direction. The problem should be set up with the wind or scent cone traveling directly toward the dog.

Repeat the above exercise on other rubble piles with a short rest in between exercises if possible. Watch the dog carefully for fatigue or frustration. A set of three exercises totals nine individual searches! Keep them simple and motivating and then end the search training for the day. Reward the dog well at the end of the session.

Continue to set up similar exercises, but vary the accessibility to the helper and increase the difficulty of the searches by lengthening the search time. Once the dog is able to search and find all of the helpers successfully, it is important to back off a little on the training and change the training format. You have asked the dog to do some serious searching which has helped to establish the work ethic in the dog, however, it is important not to burn the dog out by over training!

Remember to keep this a fun game for the dog. One way to do this is to include lots of run-aways in the training program, five run-aways for each search exercise. Run-aways do not have to be short and quick; they can be a long exercise. For example, one training session may include three or four exercises where the dog watches the helper leave. The helper may even tease the dog as he leaves, but then the dog is not allowed to go search for another 5-10 minutes and should not see where the helper hides.

CANINE PROOFING

The deployable canine needs to be prepared to deal with real world disasters. Up to this point, your training has been fairly sterile. Now, you must make an effort to provide as many distractions in the training area as possible. It is a good idea to set up distractions in the pile for that particular day and not hide any helpers until the dog has worked through the distractions. Then, a helper can do a pop-up so the dog can end the training session on a positive note. The following list of items needs to be addressed one at a time to avoid confusion in the dog. Once the dog has been exposed and proofed to the distractions, they can be added to your regular training sessions.

The Distraction List:
- Clothing/bedding/shoes/baby diapers.
- A combination of shoes, clothes, and food in the same hole.
- Workers on the pile operating tools.
- All kinds of noise from machinery and air compressors, etc.
- Caged live animals or some road killed animals.
- Consider cadaver scent and fresh blood in appropriate containers.

Food Distractions

To introduce food on the rubble pile, put it in containers and hide it in inaccessible places so that the dog cannot get it and be rewarded. The handler must know where the food is hidden so that appropriate corrections can be made, if needed. During this training period, a variety of food should be used including fish, left over foods from last night's dinner, dog food (moist and dry), and any training treat that you have used to reward the dog. The dog must understand he is working and this is not snack time.

The wise handler will do some food proofing training off of the rubble pile training first, especially if the dog is a "chow hound." The goal is for the dog to ignore all food while working, even if food is within easy grasp on the surface of the search area. The dog that has successfully completed the beginning distraction training on the alert barrel will have a foundation to build on.

Mock scenarios provide the opportunity to proof your training. Food may be scattered around the pile and be accessible to the dog. In the Oklahoma City disaster, food on the ground was a problem for many dogs. The amount of pizza and other fast food strewn on the grounds around the building was incredible.

Clothing Distractions

Place all sorts of clothing and shoes, such as sports clothes, children clothes, diapers, and blankets/bedding, on the rubble. These distractions should be placed around the pile, with some concealed within the rubble. It may be a good idea to flag the area (but not all of the time) so that the clothes can be retrieved and so the handler will know when to correct the dog, if needed.

Workers, Air Compressors, Jack Hammers and Other Tools

Many handlers or training groups do not take the time to set up problems with workmen and tools. It is important to train on the pile with workmen using power tools. You can also train in landfills or construction sites where work is being done so the dog can get used to the sight and sounds of workers and their equipment. If your Task Force Rescue Team is having a practice and it is permis-

Food is placed in containers and then hidden in the rubble.

sible, allow the dog to be around the rescue team while they are using all of the tools. If possible, have the dog search and find a concealed helper in the area. Invite the rescue team to a mock training scenario with other search dogs so you can prepare for a realistic situation.

A rescue team is working on site and the dog must search through the distraction.

INCREASING THE NUMBER OF VARIABLES

Having dealt with a series of different distractions, let's change the situation so that the dog will now need to deal with a number of variables.

The Situation List:
- No victims in the rubble.
- Two victims in the same hole but not visible to handler.
- Two victims close to each other.
- Search exercises in which the helper does not have a toy or food reward.
- Exercise the dog before the search problem (bike ride 3 miles, etc.).
- Search exercises at all times of the day and night.
- Fine (thorough) search of a difficult area.

- Directed fine search of an area.
- Direction and control exercises around taped off hazards.
- Dog searching for the helper in a taped off hazardous area.

No Victim in the Rubble

In real life, the dog will come across many situations where he has searched a rubble pile and did not find a victim. This is something that needs to be practiced during training. Each handler needs to develop a way to reward the dog for successfully searching an area, even if no victim was found. If the dog has not experienced this type of situation, it may become confused or lose motivation for future searches. When you are practicing zero victim searches, first search a blank pile, reward the dog, and then go to another pile and search for a concealed helper. Then, increase the number of zero piles, while mixing in victims in different piles, and always reward the dog for a good search. Give the dog a big paycheck at the end of training.

Two Victims in Same Hole

This exercise takes some planning and is not easy to set up, but is very necessary for the dog and handler to practice. The exercise confuses some dogs while others seem to work it out quickly. Usually, it is the handlers who are more likely to be confused if they do not have advanced warning of this type of problem. The set up is very important for the success of the exercise. It is more beneficial if it can be set up in a deep hole so that one helper can hide in a concealed position below or off to the side of the first helper. The first helper found should leave the hole while the dog is being rewarded. This gives the dog a chance to go back and alert on the second victim. It is important that someone who is aware of the situation be with the handler to prevent the handler from correcting the dog if the handler doesn't trust the dog's alert.

Two Victims Placed Close Together

This is a variation of the exercise with two victims in the same hole. However, the second victim should be placed close to the first victim, perhaps 5 to 10 feet apart, but in different holes. If the handler is unaware of the exercise, he may think that the dog is alerting on scent from the same victim in two different locations. Usually, this exercise is not as confusing to the dog as it may be for the handler. This type of scenario is a valuable training experience and a good opportunity for the handler to learn to read and trust the dog. Again, it is important for the handler to praise and reward the dog and not to make a correction.

In practice it is best to have another handler present to explain that what the dog is doing is correct if the handler seems to believe the dog is in error. This is not the time to make an error. Trust the dog unless you can confirm that he is wrong and then decide how to fix the problem.

Helper/Victim Does Not Have Toy/Food

At this point in training, the victim should not have the dog's reward, unless the problem is being set up as a motivational exercise. It is important for the dog to practice making the find with the handler presenting the reward to the helper. This will help to proof the dog from searching for the toy or food scent to help locate the victim. During testing and real deployments, the victims will not have rewards with them obviously. All of the rewards must come from the handler. However, it is important to continue emphasizing victim loyalty by keeping the dog guessing as to when the victim will have his reward.

Direction, Control, and Fine Searches of Taped Off Areas

The dog may have to search out of sight or in a taped off area. The DSD is frequently asked to search an area that is considered hazardous and off limits for the handler. Usually, the dog is allowed to freely search the taped off area. However, even during a free search, the dog will need some direction in order to stay in the area. Once the dog has done a free search, it is usually necessary to direct the dog to do a fine search of a specific area. A fine search directed from a distance takes some training and needs to be practiced. Most dogs do not pay attention to the material that defines the search area. It takes lots of practice for the dog to search under direction from the handler, so spend time on this in your training.

Teach the "Go Around" Search Technique

While searching a disaster site, directing the dog to search the perimeter of an area independent of the handler is a very useful skill. The handler should direct the dog to circle the rubble pile. In doing so, the dog has an excellent chance of picking up the scent of a victim. Of course, this technique can only be used if there is a well-defined rubble area. It would not be a safe or a wise decision to have the dog search an entire city block.

Set up the exercise so that it resembles the inaccessible victim problem. The helper should be placed on the right side of the pile close to the perimeter, midway between the front and back of the pile. The wind should be blowing across the pile from left to right. The handler stands in the taped off area and sends the dog to the right side of the pile with a hand signal and a search

The dog must be able to be directed around taped off hazardous areas.

command. The dog should not go up on the pile but should stay on the perimeter of the pile. If the dog doesn't make the turn and go down the right side of the pile, the handler needs to give more direction. As the dog travels down the side, he should detect the scent cone of the hiding helper, follow it to the helper, and alert. The helper should then come out and reward the dog all the way back to the handler.

Continue setting up exercises with the helper placed at the corner of the pile, at the back of the pile, and eventually, all the way around the pile. If the dog has any difficulty catching on to the search game, try a helper run-away around the edge of the pile. This should help engage the dog to successfully find the helper. Once the dog learns this skill, you will observe that the dog is able to search the pile more efficiently. Dogs are great at finding the path of least resistance. This quality indicates a dog that works smart; it does not mean the dog is lazy or uncomfortable on the rubble.

CONSIDER SCENT CONDITIONS IN BUILDINGS

Scent pools in buildings can be best described as a collection of scent particles contained in an area by walls or other obstructions. The scent is flowing to this area from elsewhere, and is continually being re-supplied by the source, the victim. The handler needs to be aware of this phenomenon to conduct a more effective search. It is possible that the victim is not located in the immediate area where the scent is pooling. The victim may be in a place that is being affected by the sun and atmospheric conditions that cause a chimney effect. This is where the scent is sucked straight up into the atmosphere or ceiling, carried some distance, and then deposited, forming a scent pool in another location, away from the victim.

Scent pools can develop from many causes. For instance, an area that has *very poor* air movement, such as a basement or underground tunnel, can develop a scent pool. In Austria, DSDs frequently train in factories that were bombed in World War II. Some of these buildings have incredible tunnel systems that are still intact. They are very difficult to search, as there is very little air movement and no light source, except the light that is provided by the handler. Small storage rooms branch off of the tunnels. The dogs would enter a room with a known hidden helper/person and literally stand on their hind legs barking at the ceiling and run around very frustrated. Sometimes, the hiding helper was placed against the wall just inside the door. The handler had to take charge and direct the dog to do a fine (very thorough) search to locate the victim. Many finds were made because the dog or handler stepped on or bumped into the hiding person. How is this behavior explained? What was the scent doing? The ambient temperature of the room was cold. Because cold air falls and warm air rises, the warm scent particles would rise from the hiding person, then cool and fall to the ground. If the person was hidden long enough, scent diffusion might also begin to affect the scent picture and create a large scent pool filling the whole room.

For more detailed information on scent conditions refer to Appendix B.

SIZING UP A RUBBLE PILE AND FORMING A SEARCH PLAN

Some people seem to have a talent for visualizing the most efficient way to search an area while others have to learn through experience. There are some techniques and guidelines that can help a handler to develop this skill. However, how a handler plans to search during a real scenario versus a test may be very different.

During a test, time is a limiting factor. You are a single resource and do not have the advantage of spotters who may observe the dog in an area that is not clearly visible to you. You will have to make the best of the test as it is set up for you.

In a real search, you may have the option to have a particular hazardous item or a layer of debris removed. If your dog indicates an area of interest, you can have a second dog work the area to confirm your results when you are finished. This is a big confidence booster, especially if you are several days into an incident. The second dog should always cover the area and confirm any alerts or areas of interest. Both dogs need to have a focused alert before rescue teams commit to an extrication that might possibly last 10 to 20 hours.

Most handlers begin their assignments with a free search of the area, or for inaccessible areas, send the dog on a perimeter search of the pile. The dog has an excellent chance of catching scent and locating a victim using these techniques. Once the dog has completed the initial search, the handler may direct the dog to search any areas, perhaps from a different direction, where the dog showed some interest or possibly did not cover thoroughly enough.

While the dog is searching an accessible area, the handler has an opportunity to evaluate the rubble, see various landmarks, and develop a plan of how to better search the area. It is a good idea to make a sketch map of the area at this time. It should include a North arrow, the wind direction, prominent features, and the general shape of the pile (in most incidents, the Search Team Manager will do this for the team).

Many handlers like to "double cover" a search area. They will direct the dog to perform a grid search so that the wind direction crosses the grid pattern perpendicularly, i.e., the wind is blowing N to S and the dog grids E to W. When that is complete, the handler may direct the dog in a zigzag pattern into the wind, making the pattern as fine as needed based on the time allowed and optimal scenting conditions. This technique increases the probability of detecting a victim.

It may be very difficult for a handler to pull his dog out of an area in which he has shown a lot of interest. However, removing your dog from an area of interest may prevent the dog from being pushed into a false alert. Some dogs will leave an area and then return on their own. The dog may leave the area to go search another area and then come back to the first area of interest once it has ruled out other sections to help pinpoint the location of the victim.

If the situation allows, have the dog rework an area of interest from a different direction than it was working the first time. If you have access to the area, call the dog to you, slightly restrain and refocus the dog, and then send it into the area with your search command. The dog may either discard the area, alert, or continue to be interested. If this happens, the area should be marked and another dog should search the area to confirm the results of the first dog.

KEEP YOUR DOG MOTIVATED

It is important to remember that dogs will tire after working many hours. They need motivational problems set up so they can have an *easy* find, a good reward, and an adequate rest period. This helps to keep their working drive high. In some major disaster sites where there were many casualties and few live finds, the handlers became depressed. Many handlers thought their dogs were also depressed, but that is unlikely. The dog's motivation will certainly decrease if he isn't properly rewarded. Most dogs do not have a problem finding dead bodies, especially if they have been trained to detect them. They are happy to do so because they will be rewarded. Remember, it is your responsibility as a handler to keep your dog motivated and to give opportunities for the dog to earn a reward.

11

THE FEMA ADVANCED TYPE I TEST

Once you have completed all of the training and proofing, it is time for you to plan to take the Type I Test. Plan your training days to prepare for the test two months in advance. This book includes a canine physical fitness peak performance program that you can personalize for your own training needs. See "Canine Fitness" in Appendix A.

The handler must also prepare for the test. There are some different skills and handler techniques required for the test that are not necessarily the same as what is needed in handling a dog on a real mission. Reading your dog is very important in either case, but what you do with the information you gain may be very different. Make sure you read the FEMA guidelines and performance criteria carefully.

TYPE I TEST OVERVIEW

In contrast to the Type II Test that focused on basic disaster dog search skills, the Type I Test is structured to evaluate the team's (the handler and the dog) ability to handle all aspects of a realistic disaster search operation. To successfully pass the test the team and handler must*:

- Search three separate rubble sites, each ranging from 6,000-15,000 square feet with a minimum average height of six to ten feet.
- Locate five of six victims with no more than one false alert.
- Find victims that will be well concealed from both handler and dog and encounter several false victim locations.
- Search one or more search sites that will be contaminated with distractions.

* More details and requirements are available online at www.fema.gov/usr/canine. shtm. You should download and copy all of the information on this site relating to the Type I Test. You may find the www.disasterdog.org site to be more user friendly.

- Must demonstrate the ability to establish "scene safety" through a detailed interview.
- Draw a site sketch and debrief within ten minutes after the search is concluded. The handler shall make a sketch indicating alerts, prominent features and compass orientation and a North arrow.

PRE-CERTIFICATION MOCK TEST

I recommend that you and your support group plan to run a mock test 3-4 weeks before the test date. It is important to give yourself this amount of time to correct or strengthen any problem or weakness that may be discovered. The mock test should resemble a real scenario as much as possible. A mock test will do wonders to help you keep your calm and to fine-tune any last minute issues that arise. It is very important to practice all of the handler skills and to keep the training exciting for the dog. Go to as many new or different sites as possible. Include plenty of run-away problems. Vary the person who offers the reward to the dog, so that the dog gets the reward from both you and the helper/victim. Plan how you will reward the dog during the test. Some handlers give the dog a small food reward at one victim and then a toy or tug game at the next. Make it interesting but make sure you practice the way you want to perform in the test. Don't make any last minute changes that you have not practiced.

Perhaps the most important part of testing is the handler's attitude. The ability to retain your normal decorum under pressure takes practice. You are the person the dog knows and is comfortable with. Your voice will give you away if you are nervous or not comfortable! Have your teammates set up mock tests for you that will include blank or zero victim piles, as well as other interesting scenarios that will put you on edge. They need to do their best to rattle your cage or push your buttons so that you can practice being under a high-pressure situation.

After your mock test, evaluate your performance and:
- Address any weaknesses that show up with the dog or handler.
- Do only fun things with the dog during the last week.
- Review search building marking instructions and be prepared to use them (see Appendix D).
- Review making a sketch map of each of your search sites.
- Review handler interview process. See the "Cheat Sheet" in Appendix E.
- Remember to provide a search plan and to inform the evaluators of any modifications.
- Practice doing safety/wellness checks on your dog.

TAKING THE TYPE I TEST

You and the dog will be tested using the criteria from FEMA's Type I Disaster Search Canine Readiness Evaluation Process. As the handler, you must familiarize yourself with all of the performance requirements. These guidelines establish the criteria that evaluators must adhere to in order to determine whether you will pass or fail. It will give you an overall understanding of the importance of each exercise and what the evaluators expect to see. With that said, let's review the keys to your team passing the test:

- The handler must demonstrate the ability to direct the dog and the dog must show responsiveness to the handler.
- The handler must conduct a site assessment interview and develop a search plan.
- The dog must search and perform a focused bark alert, independent of the handler, finding five of the six victims.
- The handler must describe and draw a sketch map of each search site and debrief at the end of each search.
- The handler must complete a safety/wellness check on the dog at the conclusion of each search.

There will be three rubble sites and each has different search parameters. The three sites may consist of all the same kind of material or each pile may be different. A rubble pile with vegetated waste may be particularly difficult for the dog as are piles consisting largely of wood, so the dog should have been exposed to training on each before the test is taken.

There will be a possible zero to three victims hidden in each of the three sites. One site will be completely inaccessible and the handler will not able to see the dog work. When the dog demonstrates a focused bark alert, the handler may go to the alert, mark it, and decide if they will stay at this alert site or return to the starting point. One search site will have perimeter access and one high point. The handler may direct the dog as needed from the perimeter and the dog must locate the victims. The handler is permitted to mark the victim location and then return to the perimeter or the high point. At the third search site, the handler will have full access to the whole site. The test sites will have false holes, food and animal distractions as well as noise distraction such as running generators or other equipment. As the Type I Test is currently written and evaluated, a team will fail if the handler does not examine a dog that falls on the site, request decontamination of the dog if it gets into known or suspicious water or material, or fails to do a safety check at the completion of each search site.

A rubble pile consisting of vegetated waste materials.

A rubble pile consisting of wood pallets and construction materials.

A handler conducts a canine safety check after a test.

Disaster Site Interview

At the disaster test site, you will be expected to gather information to maintain the safety of you, your dog, and your teammates from the officials at the scene. Your life and your dog's life could be at stake. The answers to these questions will also give you valuable information to help in developing an efficient search plan. There is an Interview "Cheat Sheet" in Appendix E to which you can refer. It is designed so you can copy and laminate it so you can wear it with your identification tags. It is permissible and advisable to use it in the test or on a real mission. The disaster interview that follows is not an exact replica of the Interview Check List, but is divided into two segments to encourage you think about safety issues and search issues as you would need to on a real mission.

Safety Issues

- Has a Structural Engineer checked the building? Is it safe for handler to enter?
- Where is the safe entry?
- Has the building been checked for hazardous materials?
- Utilities: What and how were they secured? Water? Gas? Electric?

Search Issues
- When did the incident/collapse occur?
- What type of building and how many people did it contain?
- How many people are missing?
- Has it been searched and by whom?
- What did they find?
- Were casualties found? How were the locations of the casualties marked?
- Are there blueprints available? How many floors were in the building? Was there a basement? Elevators? Cafeteria? Restrooms? Break room?
- What support teams are available? Task Force? Heavy Rescue? Fire Department? Medical? On-call Veterinarian?

It is very important to understand the safety issues associated with each disaster site. The safety issues must be answered to your satisfaction or you should not proceed with the search. A concrete building that has pancaked or has been reduced to a rubble pile is not as big a concern as a partially collapsed building. The handler must be aware of hanging debris or objects, unstable or leaning walls, un-reinforced masonry walls, or fireplace chimneys that may collapse.

Utilities are also extremely important. In a large area of destruction, the utility company may initially turn off the electricity to a specific grid (area) and then turn it back on again. If there are energized wires in your search area, it could be very dangerous. Be sure that the electricity is turned off at the site as well as the general area. The fire department calls this procedure "Locked out and tagged out," which means that a specific fireman has locked out (shut off) and tagged out (secured) the area, so that if the electricity is turned on again, this particular building will not be energized accidentally.

This is important for the safety of the search. Be sure that you are comfortable with the interview process and use the "Cheat Sheet." It lists all of the important information contained on the evaluator's score sheet and in the same order. This way, you will not get confused or skip an important question. You must ask each question in order to pass the test. Pay attention to the scenario given to you. While it may be silly, it often contains important information that you will need in order to formulate a search plan.

Search Building Marking
Practice using the techniques for marking a building that has been searched and keep a chart with you for reference. First, you must make a slash mark and put the name of the search unit. Once your search is complete and everyone is out of

the building, draw the second slash mark and list any hazards in the right quadrant, victims that were found dead or alive in the bottom quadrant, and the time and date everyone left the building in the top quadrant. The diagram in Appendix D shows the results of the search.

Structure/Hazard Assessment

People often confuse the Structural/Hazards Assessment with Search Building Marking. It is important to know the difference. The Structural/Hazards Assessment is done by the engineers and specifically deals with the safety and stability of the building. There will be a large orange box by the main entrance. If there are no markings in the box, it is safe to search. If there is a slash mark diagonally from one corner to the other it is probably OK to search but the building contains hazards. If there is an "X" in the box, it is not safe to enter the building. The dog should do a perimeter search and check any voids that are accessible but the handler must stay out of this area! The diagram in Appendix D shows an assessment of the structural hazards at a hypothetical site.

Reading Your Dog

If the dog is interested in a specific area, you must read the dog's body language to determine if this is due to a food distraction, an animal, a minute scent of a deep burial, or uncertainty caused by the fatigue. In practice, a common training technique is to recall the dog, face the area of interest, put the leash or collar around the dog's neck, and restrain the dog as you use your voice to excite the dog. Then, you release the dog with a hand signal directed towards the area of interest. While this is good technique in training and for a real mission, you won't be able to do this during a test. The evaluator is interested in whether or not you can read your dog. During a testing situation, the dog must alert independent of the handler. The handler cannot precipitate or coach an alert and to do so is cause for failure. The wise handler will direct the dog away from the area of interest and rework the area by approaching from a different direction. In many cases, the dog will alert on his own as he nears the area from a different angle, even if physically tired. Sometimes, taking a step or two closer to the dog is all the reinforcement a tired dog may need to alert, giving a focused bark that indicates the presence of live human scent. A focused bark is a repetitive bark, which most evaluators define as at least three barks before the handler gives any verbal support.

Mapping Skills

This is an important skill that is needed for the test. Teams have failed for providing inadequate maps. The map that you make of your search assignment and the location of your dog's alerts are very important. It should contain enough detail and landmarks so that a search team manager can find your alert area, even if there is no flagging tape marking it. Most handlers may not see distinguishing landmarks when flagging an alert area because they have not trained themselves to look for landmarks! Take a minute to look around at the surrounding rubble and look for landmarks to use in making the map. Practice this every time your dog alerts when you go to reward your dog. Some handlers may even make a quick sketch of the alert site. Be sure to use the correct symbols on your map, i.e., **V** for suspected victim and **V** with a circle around it for a *confirmed* victim. A confirmed victim is one you can see, have heard make a verbal response, or which two dogs have alerted on indicating a live person. In a test situation, the victims are instructed not to reply, but upon occasion, someone may forget.

There are two simple techniques that you can use to draw maps. One method is to divide the search site into four sections. The division line can go north to south and west to east or from one outstanding feature to another. There must be some defining feature to use for the division lines or this will not work. Decide where in the quadrant(s) your dog alerted and estimate or pace off the distance to the boundaries, giving at least three directions. It is helpful if you can include a landmark for each quadrant as well. The map must contain details and points of reference, a North arrow, wind direction, and an estimated percentage of how well you covered the search area, often referred to as probability of detection (POD). Clearly mark any areas that you feel were not searched by your dog.

Another way to draw a map uses the unique landmarks of the site. Include any prominent features, high points, and flat areas and mark which direction is north. Then, estimate the distance from the nearest boundary and any unique landmarks relative to the alert area. Include the wind direction, percent of search area covered, and all areas that *were not* searched by the dog. If you have good landmarks, this method may be a good choice for designing your sketch, although you should practice both ways of drawing the map. Regardless of the method you choose to make your map, it must contain enough physical features and reference points for the search manager or rescue team to find the location of where the dog alerted.

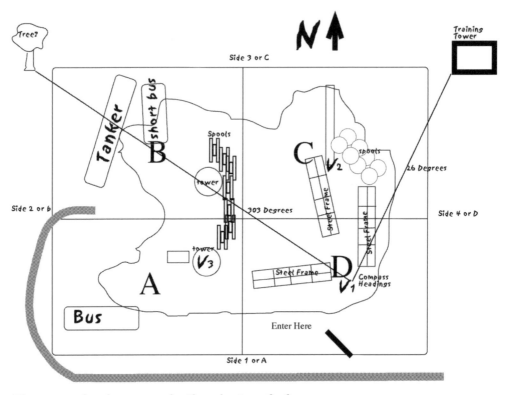

The map needs to have many details and points of reference.

Canine Safety Check

Remember to offer the dog water on every search site and more often as needed. Some handlers forget to water the dog or to take care of themselves. Detailed searching dries the mucous membranes in the dog's nose, which causes the dog to require more water. It is imperative for you to keep the dog and yourself hydrated throughout the search.

Make it a habit to check the dog from head to toe after each search problem, paying special attention to the feet. If you run your hands over the dog's body, you will quickly discover any bleeding from a cut or puncture wound. Most dogs are so focused on the search that they do not react to small wounds. Nevertheless, any wounds should be cleaned and attended to.

Handlers need to be very aware of hazards. You and your dog are valuable resources and you need to protect both of you. Assume that there will be hazards such as chemicals, crushed gas cans, razor sharp metal flashing, or broken glass partitions that the dog may not be able to see in a building. Check your dog often and be especially aware of the dog's eyes, which may need flushing. The dog's feet are extremely vulnerable to all of the hazards associated with a rubble site. If you suspect that your dog has come in contact with any hazardous materials, report this information immediately and get help. Don't wait until you are through searching an area. It is better to be safe than sorry! A team will fail if the handler does not examine a dog that falls on the site, request decontamination of the dog if he gets into known or suspicious water/ material, or fails to do a safety check at the completion of each search site.

Debriefing

After completing a search at a rubble site, either for a test or a real incident, you will be expected to explain exactly what areas your dog searched, where the alerts were located, and any areas of interest. You will be asked to give a POD or a rough estimate of the percentage of the area(s) you covered and to sketch a map. Each section of the areas that you search should have a corresponding POD. Include any areas that *were not* searched by the dog. This information is very beneficial to the search team manager in assessing what has been completed and what still needs to be done. It is important to include other pertinent information about the site that may not have been known previously, such as low air movement and any hazards that may be present.

One of the most important parts of the debriefing session is the *follow-up* recommendations of the handler. Should this site be searched again by another dog or at a different time of day? Based on the handler's knowledge of the site, recommendations should be given as to whether the site needs to be searched again in the future.

Good luck in testing and in your real time searches. You should be prepared if you have followed the training outlined in this book. Have confidence in yourself and most importantly, trust your dog!

12

READY FOR DEPLOYMENT

Once you have passed the Type I Test, you are now considered to be a "mission ready team" and you must be ready for deployment at any time. Each Task Force has its own procedures for DSD teams to join. Some have a training program and others will hold a "try out day" for beginning and intermediate teams and some only consider DSD teams that are ready to test and have passed a "Pre-Test" (a non-official test that contains all the elements of a FEMA Canine Readiness Evaluation.)

In 2006 the Type II Test will be eliminated and replaced by a Task Force sponsored "Skills Assessment" process that will include all of the skills of the Type II Test. The Type II skills training set forth in this book will prepare you for this process. Each Task Forse is sponsored by a state agency or organization within a state and is a resource for that state. They must meet the requirements of the FEMA US&R Response System. If a national disaster is declared by the President, those Task Forces become FEMA Task Forces and are deployed.

There may be opportunities to serve with your trained Disaster Search Dog whether or not you receive the Type I certification and whether or not you choose to join a FEMA Task Force. State and local government entities through-out the country recognize the value of the trained DSD and have a variety of programs that you might be able to participate in ranging from formal to less formal. In California, for example, the state Office of Emergency Services is in the process of providing a certification process for Type III and IV Disaster Search Dogs for use in local incidents with less rigorous requirements than the FEMA program. In many towns and cities, the local fire department maintains a list of trained dogs and handlers that they can call upon if need be. You should contact your local agency charged with emergency response to find out what kind of opportunities may exist.

FEMA TASK FORCE ORGANIZATION

Once you are assigned to a Task Force you will be given an orientation class to familiarize yourself with the Task Force and your role in it. You will be issued a Field Operations Guide (FOG), a very important book. It is sort of the "Bible" of search operations, containing position descriptions, search strategy and tactics, rescue operations and many other topics. Each member of a Task Force receives specialized training pertinent to his or her job. The Canine Search Specialist Handler receives training in the following courses: Canine Search Specialist School (40 Hours), Incident Command System (ICS 100 & 200, the systems used to run a search), Confined Space Awareness, Hazmat Awareness, Structure Safety, Rescue Systems I (40 hours), First Aid, and CPR. In addition, Canine Search Specialist Handlers must pass the Task Force physical fitness exam and the Weapons of Mass Destruction (WMD) awareness courses.

Whenever an emergency occurs, one or more Task Forces, replete with the necessary tools, equipment, and requisite skills, can be deployed by FEMA to natural or man-made disaster sites. When activated, each Task Force must respond with all its personnel and equipment at the point of departure within six hours of activation.

Currently, there are 28 FEMA US&R Task Forces spread throughout the continental United States that are trained and equipped to handle structural collapse. A Task Force is typically comprised of about 70 members (it used to be 64, but with the emphasis on WMDs six more hazardous material positions have been added) and is divided into four major functional elements: Search and Rescue, Planning, Logistics, and Medical. Task Force members include structural engineers and specialists in hazardous materials, heavy rigging, logistics, communications, rescue, medical and, of course, search. The search component includes handlers and Disaster Search Dogs, collectively referred to as Canine Search Specialists. By design, on a deployment, there are two Task Force members assigned to each position for the rotation and relief of personnel. This allows for round-the-clock Task Force operational shifts of twelve hours on and twelve hours off.

Before the Task Force arrives at the incident, an Advance Team or a local Triage Team will have evaluated the site and made Task Force assignments. When the Task Force arrives, they will set up a base camp and prepare to become operational. The Task Force may divide immediately into "A" and "B" shifts. The "A" shift will begin working and the "B" shift will be the initial resting team, each team working twelve hour shifts. This was the schedule at the World Trade Center in New York. In very large events where the need for many Task Forces is indicated, both shifts may be deployed at the same time, as they were in the Oklahoma City bombing. The initial response was a "blitz" for 18 hours and then shifted to the 12 hours on and 12 hours off. The search component of the Task Force is composed of four dogs and their handlers, two Technical Search Specialists, two Hazmat Specialists and the two Search Team Managers. Each

Task Force will have its own way of determining which dogs will be deployed. Some prefer to send two veteran Type I canine teams and two new Type I canine teams. Others have a lottery of sorts. Some Task Forces do not have enough trained DSDs to choose all Type I teams and will send their most experienced Type II teams.

READY TO DEPLOY

Before you are called is the time to pack your bags and be ready. If you get the call, be sure to read the Field Operations Guide and take it with you. Report to the staging point on time. While the Task Force will provide gear, be sure to have your handler's pack filled with gear you might need for up to 36 hours. It goes with you wherever you travel. Many times, when the Task Force arrives at the destination, the packs and gear may not arrive at the same time. So you will need your 24-36 hour pack. In addition, each canine handler is allowed 60 lbs of gear for themselves and 40 additional lbs for the dog. This usually does not include dog food, as that will be part of the canine "cache" which the Task Force provides. The list below contains a few items that are a must to have with you when you deploy:

- Your dog.
- Any prescriptions that you or the dog must take.
- Food for yourself such as protein bars, dry fruit, snack food, and some water in your pack.
- Food for your dog and a collapsible dish that can be used for water or food in your pack.
- Small wallet with some cash and credit card.
- Camera, notebook and pencil/pen.
- Toothbrush and toothpaste.
- Be ready for your "out the door" medical check that will be performed by the Task Force doctor to make sure you are not ill. This includes taking a base line temperature, blood pressure, a check of any prescriptions, and DNA swabs for identification if needed.
- Have your papers with you for canine check in; include the dates of canine rabies vaccination and other immunizations.
- If flying, have a quick release harness with you, as some air transportation regulations require the dog to be tethered during the flight.

When you arrive at the facility where you will be housed, the first job will be to set up sleeping quarters for you and the dogs. In most deployments, the canine teams have a section to themselves. This is helpful as it give the dogs some privacy and a better chance to rest.

The next big task is to help unpack the Task Force supplied cache and separate out the tools and supplies that will need to be moved to the forward Base of Operations (BO) near your Task Force assignment. The tools and supplies need to be arranged within the BO.

The team normally divides into a #1 Team and a #2 Team, each expected to be on a 12-hour work shift. On a typical day, one might get up at 5:30 AM to feed and care for the dog and eat breakfast. Then you will be bussed to the site. When you arrive at the at the search site, the Search Team Manager, Hazmat Specialist, Technical Search Specialist, and Canine Search Specialist will survey the site and determine the best search strategy for the assigned operation. Then search operations begin in the assigned area with one dog searching at a time. Work would typically end at 7 PM when the #2 Team would take over.

Deployment search plan considerations:

- Understand your assignment.
- Determine your assigned search area.
- Wear whatever personal protection equipment you are required to have such as the full-face mask respirators.
- Look for search marking and building assessment markings.
- Consider air movement when deploying the dogs.
- Consider temperature, time of day, weather.
- Consider permeability of construction materials.
- Minimize exposure to hazards.
- Confirm alerts with a second dog.
- Determine if a detailed grid search is needed.
- Consider re-searching under more favorable conditions.
- Debrief and summarize canine search of area assigned, make recommendations for next search, provide a detailed map as requested.
- Check your dog for injuries after every search.
- Decontaminate canine and handler if necessary.
- Hydrate handler and dog frequently.

A TYPICAL SEARCH OPERATION

The Canine Team #1 will typically be deployed to free search the sector the Task Force has determined to be the first priority. If there are no alerts, the handler will then direct the dog to either perform a fine search or a more open grid search (described below) of the sector. Any area where the dog showed interest will usually be carefully re-searched in a fine grid. Usually the Search Team Manager (STM) and other team members will act as observers. Sometimes another Canine Team Handler will also observe, however usually the other handler and DSD will be resting. Observers should be positioned to watch from different vantage points. The observers provide the handler with important information on how well the area is covered, areas that need to be re-covered, and any subtle canine body language that may indicate a possible victim who is buried very deep.

If Canine Team #1 detects human scent and alerts, the handler will mark the area. The STM will direct the team to finish searching the sector or leave the sector so that Canine Team # 2 can be deployed into the area for confirmation. Before Canine Team #2 is deployed, the alert is documented and the potential victim marking removed. If the alert is confirmed by Canine Team #2, it will be flagged, marked on the map and the STM will inform the Task Force leader of a confirmed find.

When Canine Team #1 has completed the sector, or searched 20-30 minutes depending on the temperature, humidity, or other factors, the canine teams will switch. Canine Team #2 will begin free searching from a different direction to increase the probability of detection. The STM will decide if Canine Team #2 needs to do a grid search. The STM, if it is decided that a grid search is desirable, will most likely direct the team to perform a grid search in the opposite direction than Canine Team #1 to increase the probability of detection.

If the whole Task Force is working together, then Canine Teams #1 and #2 may be deployed at the same time in sectors next to each. If there are more teams available, Teams #3 and #4 will be the confirmation teams. Both STMs will be observing the dogs search. When the search of a sector by both dogs is complete, the teams will switch sectors and so on until the assignment is complete. Continued researching of any structure, as it is penetrated by cutting and removal, is important in order to better locate the initial victim and provide information regarding additional victims.

TYPICAL SEARCH PATTERNS

A fine search grid is utilized in high probability areas of finding victims because it yields the best chance of detection. A more open grid pattern may be utilized in an area with a low probability of containing victims or due to constraints that limit the amount of time that can be committed to a search area. Search patterns in an enclosed building need to be methodical and complete. Buildings typically vary depending on the floor plan and number of hallways. If it is a simple floor plan, the team will start to the right and stay right until they have covered the whole floor. When they have completed the floor and are reassigned, a second team may enter and go left and stay left to the end of the search for double coverage. This increases the probability of detection. If a simultaneous search is desired, they may begin searching at the same time with one team going right and one team going left.

As always, check your dog carefully at the end of each search to avoid more serious injuries from developing due to lack of attention. Keeping you, the handler, and the dog hydrated is also very important. However, every time you need to drink you have to remove your respirator, and that can break the seal and reduces the effectiveness of the respirator. It is a two-edge sword, you must drink and there isn't time to leave the pile every time you need water.

The best working conditions for the search dogs is normally at dawn and dusk. At these times of day scent is generally rising or is stable and accessible to the dog, the weather is cooler, and winds are usually lighter. The least productive working conditions are during the heat of the day, when strong winds blow the scent all over, or in heavy rain. It is more difficult and less effective for the dog to work in temperatures of 90 degrees or more. They can only work short periods of time and require large quantities of water to stay hydrated. The mucus membranes dry out in the scenting process. Sometimes a small spritzer bottle to spray the nose is very effective.

Deploying the dog in a free search is a very effective search. The dog can cover large sectors in a relatively short period of time. However, the handler has a responsibility to direct the dog when needed to cover an area adequately. To get the best probability of detection the dog must free search and then perform a grid search. Keep in mind the temperature when searching. If it is hot the search period will be short. Some dogs work best if they have short search periods and short rests. Other dogs can search effectively for an hour without a break. The handler must know what works best for his or her dog. Keep in mind that if the dog is not detecting live finds, it is your responsibility to set up motivational live finds for the dog once or twice a day. Your dog is your resource and you need to take the best care of him that you can.

13

ON THE SCENE AT
THREE MAJOR DISASTERS

As you continue your Disaster Search Dog training, I hope that learning about some of my real-life experiences at some of the world's worst disasters will be both inspirational and instructive. Remember, while not all DSD teams have the opportunity to work at a major disaster site, your skills and willingness to be deployed will make the world a safer place. Any DSD work you do will have a profound impact on those you help as well as yourself.

MEXICO CITY EARTHQUAKE, 1985

Twenty years makes a big difference in the evolution of disaster response. The American disaster dog teams that responded to the Mexico City earthquake in 1985 were ill-prepared by today's standards. Many of them had trained on rubble and a few had some basic disaster awareness skills, however there were many handlers who had very little training and had to rely on the training of their wilderness area search dogs. It was a miracle that none of the dogs or handlers received any injuries or killed—as many other volunteer rescue personnel were.

The teams were transported to Mexico City by a US Military C-141 and were transported home on a Military C-130 Cargo plane. The Embassy and the US Government had to get special permission from the Mexican Government in order for the military planes to fly into Mexico City.

The team was met by US Embassy Staff and transported to the Embassy. The staff had made arrangements for the handlers to stay at the Sheraton Palace Hotel and the dogs were to be housed in the Embassy basement. The teams had come prepared with sleeping bags and camping equipment. The handlers immediately decided that they didn't want to be separated from their dogs and elected to stay in the Embassy basement with the dogs. At that point, new arrangements were made and the handlers and dogs stayed at the hotel together. This was very appreciated, especially since the handlers and dogs put in long days searching. The hotel was functioning well and had survived the earthquake with only a little cosmetic damage. Staying at the hotel was especially good emotionally for the handlers. This enabled them to leave the rubble field, return to the hotel, shower, eat in the dining room, and sleep in comfortable beds. Many of the handlers had never seen a dead body in a traumatic setting. Residing in the hotel under somewhat normal living conditions helped to reduce both handler and canine stress.

The sizes of the rubble piles used to train the dogs were miniscule in comparison to the huge concrete rubble masses that confronted the dogs in Mexico. We found that concrete dust became a health hazard to both the handlers and dogs. The dogs suffered irritation to both their noses and eyes. The handlers quickly learned that it was extremely important to hydrate the dogs and themselves, to wash/spray the mucus membranes of the nose, and to pay attention to the eyes. The dogs' eyes were irrigated and soothing ointment applied at night. The handlers also began using surgical facemasks to help filter out some of the dust that they were breathing.

Each building that had collapsed was assigned a local city official to be in charge. The Army had assigned soldiers to guard each of the collapsed buildings from looters. These soldiers were armed with M1 rifles and most seemed to be very young men, if not boys. They were there to do a job but they were not very cooperative with search teams moving in and out of a search area.

When a search team received an assignment, they would travel in a Volkswagen buses to the assigned site. The addresses were often confusing, as many of the street names were repeated in different parts of the city. Often, when a team did arrive at the search site, a search would already be in progress by some other country's SAR resources.

Some of the European teams were complete teams composed of search, rescue, and medical personnel. However, there did not seem to be a system in place to coordinate the teams of the different countries. The only means of communication was by hand-held radios and the frequencies were often jammed.

When a search team received a search assignment, they were told to mark the area according to this plan: one colored strip of flagging tape for areas of potential deceased; two colored strips of flagging tape for areas of interest, but no alert; and three colored strips of flagging tape for potential live victim finds. Once the team finished the search, they would get into the VW Bus and drive to another site. The team leaders would report the teams' findings to the Embassy Staff and it would get passed to the proper authority. There was little to no feedback of when or if any rescue teams ever went to the sites that had been searched. That was the most difficult part of the experience for most handlers, not knowing if the people were ever rescued alive or dead.

Cinnamon searching a Public Works Office in Mexico City.

Our search team received an assignment to search a clothing factory. One of the volunteer workers had been crawling through the building and heard noises that he didn't think were related to the earthquake. My dog Cinnamon and I were elected to do the search, as we were the smallest members of the team. Workers had cut a hole in the roof of this building that was "pancaked" from the earthquake. The hole in the roof was about 4 feet wide and approximately 12-15 feet deep. This represented seven stories of the building. Getting to the roof presented a problem. A cage of sorts was welded together. Cinnamon and I got into the cage that was attached to a cable and lifted by crane to the top of the building. There wasn't a ladder or ropes, so I had to climb down the hole using the rebar and gaps in the concrete for footing. Cinnamon was handed from one worker to another down this shaft while I waited at the bottom to receive her.

I had a brief conversation, mostly sign language, with the man who was my guide to the search area. He didn't speak English but understood some. Together, we began crawling through the debris. At one point, we experienced an aftershock. This was the first aftershock of which I was truly conscious. I know there must have been others but I just blocked them out of my mind. We stopped

Dog and handler being lifted to the top of the clothing factory.

moving as the dust and small debris rained down on us. This was a significant aftershock and I had some serious thoughts for my safety. When all had quieted, we continued crawling to the area that Cinnamon was to search.

I knew that we had arrived in the right area when Cinnamon, who had been following behind me, suddenly pushed out in front. There was a definite change in her body language. She had detected scent and was already trying to pinpoint the location. She tried to get into one area but could not get around all of the crushed concrete that was blocking her ability to penetrate. So, she began barking and trying to dig at this one area. I tried to radio to my team that we had an alert, but they couldn't receive the transmission. I marked the area where Cinnamon was trying to dig and then we crawled back to the entrance of the hole. I climbed out and Cinnamon was lifted up from one worker to another until we reached the top. The alert was reported and then we were assigned another location to search. Much later on when we were at the airport preparing to leave, one of the Embassy staff members sent a radio communications that workers had made contact with live people in the factory. There was a big shout of joy from the team involved in that search. Finally, we had confirmation of at least some live finds that would be rescued.

It seemed like everyone worked or helped in the recovery efforts in some way. The majority of the workers had very few resources; many were without adequate tools, gloves, boots, or helmets. It was extremely labor intensive, as workers only had hammers and hacksaw blades to break through the concrete and to cut the rebar. The Mexican people were so wonderful and supportive of our efforts. They had so little and yet they offered all of the search and rescue teams food and gifts as a thank you for coming to help find the earthquake victims. The dogs were also seen as heroes. I will always remember a young boy, approximately eight years old, who offered a basket of fruit to me if I would allow him to take my dog Cinnamon for a walk and photograph the two of them together. Many of the American volunteers left Mexico City resolving to make a difference in Urban Search and Rescue in the United States. They saw the need to develop an organized team approach for incident response. They were determined to develop skilled teams in search, rescue, medical, and support management within a structured organization. This led to many meetings, brain storming, and eventually to the birth of the Federal Emergency Management Agency and the Urban Search & Rescue Response System.

THE ALFRED P. MURRAH FEDERAL BUILDING, OKLAHOMA CITY

On April 19, 1995, the bombing of the federal building in Oklahoma City shocked the nation and the world. FEMA responded with the system they had developed for just such an emergency. The Governor of Oklahoma requested help from the President of the United States, and as such, the President declared the Oklahoma incident a disaster and Task Forces were deployed to the bombing site. Arizona TF-1 was the nearest and the first to respond. From Sacramento, California TF-7 was the next team on site.

This was the first real test of the newly developed response system that was essentially born out of the destruction and frustration of the unorganized response to the Mexico City Earthquake in 1985.

The response system that had been implemented, the courses and techniques developed to train the different specialists, and the millions of dollars of state-of-the-art equipment purchased all paid off in Oklahoma City. An improved communications systems and training exercises held in advance helped the whole Task Force to develop a better working relationship among the various specialists working at the site.

The emotional response of the search and rescue personnel involved in Oklahoma City was very different than in Mexico. The Mexico City incident was due to an earthquake, a natural disaster. No one was to blame, although the earthquake killed and injured many. The Oklahoma incident was a man-made disaster, a political statement that killed and injured many innocent people, including children. The emotional tone of the community and the rescuers was one of disbelief and anger. It was difficult for some to endure. Great bonds between searchers were formed during this tragedy; many remain long-lasting as they shared an incredible experience together.

California TF-7, of which I was part, arrived on site at 11:30 pm. We had been transported by military airplane from Travis Air Force Base, California to Tinker Air Forces Base, Oklahoma. We were bussed to the site and as we approached, smoke, dust, and the bank of lights that were illuminating the building caused an eerie, radiant glow. The site was lit up like a movie set, with all of the lights exposing a huge gaping hole in the back of the building. Upon closer examination, the exterior walls on that side of the building were all missing. It resembled a child's dollhouse in which you can see all of the floors and furnishings, with a big gaping hole carved where the bomb blast occurred.

Our accommodations were at the Southwestern Bell offices. This building was about a block from the target building and it had only received cosmetic damage. Our host was most accommodating and gave us a whole floor to spread out and make ourselves as comfortable as possible. The dogs and handlers occupied two different offices spaces, spreading sleeping bags and pads on the floor for a makeshift home. We were allowed to use the executive shower, which was great, and our host very kindly arranged a laundry service for us. Especially touching was that whenever our laundry was returned, it contained several notes or drawings from children.

Stations for eye irrigation and decontamination were set up to rid the dogs of dust in their eyes and contaminants on their coats. After each search, the dogs were rinsed, scrubbed with soap, and rinsed again. Eventually a kennel dryer was also available to help dry the long-coated dogs.

Our TF started work the next morning at 6 am and worked for 18 hours. This first day at the site was a critical time for saving lives and everyone was working under adrenalin power. The dogs had lots of searching to accomplish and in many cases, they were performing a re-search of an area after some of the rubble had been removed. The search team did not have a lot of down time. However, whenever we were on a standby basis, the dogs received lots of attention. Because there was so much anger, emotion, and frustration, many search and rescue personnel stopped by to spend time with and pet the dogs. In a sense, they each took on a therapy dog role.

There was lots of rubble to search and in some areas it was quite difficult. There were some voids in places, but not like what is seen in an earthquake. There were few live humans to find so the handlers had to keep the dogs motivated to search by setting up mock problems with live victims. The dogs were all happy to have a find and get rewarded. Most of the injured victims were found in the first few hours and got out under their own power or were helped out by emergency personnel. A girl named Brandy, who was rescued from the rubble between 9 and 10 pm of the first day, was the only live victim to be rescued at a later point in time in this disaster. However, we did continue our mission to try to find and rescue live victims so our search efforts continued for over a week.

Spice searching a void in the Murrah Building close to where the bomb was exploded

The injuries to our TF team, dog and human, were all simple first aid injuries. One dog did require a few stitches on the top of a front paw that had been cut by a broken glass office partition. The dog walked right through this space and did not see that it was glass, or rather, had been a glass partition. The wound was sutured and wrapped and the dog was back to work with little lost work time.

THE WORLD TRADE CENTER, NEW YORK CITY

On September 11, 2001, terrorists piloting two commercial jet airplanes crashed into the twin towers at the World Trade Center in New York causing them to collapse.

I was part of the California Task Force 3 (TF-3), sponsored by the Menlo Park Fire Protection District. We left for New York a week later at 6 AM on the 19th of September from Travis Air Force Base. Our plane carried $2 million dollars worth of equipment in addition to 62 Task Force members and 4 dogs. We landed at McGinnis Air Force Base in New Jersey and the team was bussed to Jacob Javits Convention Center at 1:30 AM on the 20th of September.

Interestingly enough, our first assignment was not to work the WTC site but to staff and outfit a Rapid Response Team (RRT) and be available to respond to any emergencies within other parts of New York. This was because the city had lost so many of their RRT workers and emergency response vehicles in the collapse of the towers. While the WTC disaster was obviously the highest priority, we were told that New York City typically has close to 300 collapsed buildings in a year and local authorities realized that they had to rebuild their resources to deal with any event that might occur elsewhere in the city. We divided the TF into two RRTs and were stationed in various parts of New York City for three days, at which time another TF relieved us.

Then we were assigned to work at the World Trade Center (WTC) disaster site. The Task Force was split up to work a 12-hour day shift and a 12-hour night shift. My dog Sunny and I were assigned to the day shift along with a teammate named Jeff Place and his dog Zack (a male chocolate Labrador). Pat Grant and Topper (Belgian Tervuren) and Carol Herse and Teka (a yellow Labrador) were on the night shift.

On the first day of our assignment to the WTC, we were bussed to within 10 blocks of the site and walked into the site from that point. By then, the streets had been cleared of rubble and the surrounding buildings looked like stage props. When we arrived at the site, our first job was to set up our base of operations. Then the search team, consisting of the two dogs and handlers, a hazmat technician, search team manager, and a structural specialist were deployed. It's difficult to convey the enormity of this catastrophe. Compared to the Oklahoma City bombing, which involved just one building, the collapse of the towers was overwhelming. The WTC involved about 14 acres and many buildings, all tangled in a mess of steel and powder. There was very little concrete rubble of any size because so much of it had been vaporized in the fire and subsequent collapse. We were assigned to a portion of the site that had been cleared of a lot of the debris, however there was still a large amount of tangled steel to negotiate. The canine agility skills that are required and emphasized in this book really paid off for the disaster dogs and handlers. Even though the dogs had never come into contact with this kind of tangled mess, they all performed very well, relying on their foundation training.

All the personnel at the site were required to wear respiratory gear, which makes communication with the dogs very difficult. It bothered many of the handlers that we had to wear respiratory protection and the dogs could not. I had concerns that I might be shortening my dog's life by subjecting him to the toxins and dust in the air.

There was also a great deal of noise, making it difficult to talk to teammates. Many of the rescue personnel used earpiece receivers for their radio communications. The vibrations from all of the excavators, huge cranes, front loaders, and trucks were very noticeable and somewhat distracting at first. The rubble trembled continuously, sort of like a small earthquake after-shock that never ends.

I was fortunate in that the area I was assigned to work did not have any flames flare up while I was working. In some areas where a column was removed, there would often be a release of hot smoke and flames. The Fire Department aerial trucks would go into action immediately to bring it under control. Then the Hazmat folks would go in and check the quality of the air before we were allowed to go back to work.

It was during down times that my dog Sunny (a 95 pound Doberman) did some of his most important work—that of being a therapy dog. There was something about a big black male dog that made it easier for the firemen to come and give him a hug or a pat on the back. Many times, they never said a word to me but would spend a few quiet minutes with Sunny, leaving with a tear on their cheeks. Sunny is a very friendly dog and would lean into the guys as they petted him. Sunny and Zack were requested to visit the firemen at break time almost every day we were there. It was an emotional roller coaster for me, but I was very conscious of how important this contact was for this very tired, hard working crew.

Sunny and Zack are both trained to find the living. At one point in time, a "clear the area" was signaled, while a dumpster was being removed by a large crane. We were standing by and as soon as the dumpster was cleared my Search Team manager directed us to start searching. I gave Sunny the search command and Sunny started his search pattern soon letting out a huge roar of barks and, of course, we all got excited. It was a live find, but it was only one of the rescue team members in a void. However this was great for Sunny and very motivating. Sunny was not a trained as a cadaver dog, but he was able to show me, through changes in his body posture, every place from which a body had been removed and where some human bodies were still hidden in the rubble. He didn't have a trained alert for that—and he wasn't sure how to tell me about what he was finding or even if he should tell me—but I was able to read his body language to know what he had scented.

Another day, Sunny was requested to search an area that a rescue team had just cleared of tangled metal using cutting torches. Sunny searched the area and returned to one spot over and over again. I assumed that Sunny's great interest in this area was a residual live scent pool from the rescue team. I called Sunny out and he started to come, but then he turned and went back to the same place and started to dig. Later that day as I was going to lunch, a fireman came up and put his hand on my shoulder and said that Sunny was right. They recovered a brother fireman where Sunny was digging.

Sunny indicating human remains in the rubble.

Sunny and I both returned home without any injuries, for which I'm thankful. My husband David served as Lead Structural Engineer, Incident Overhead Team, for the effort and his expertise helped to minimize injuries, most of which very minor. Safety of the rescue personnel is one part of his job. Providing information and overseeing the TF engineers to ensure that they were all on the same sheet of music and were working together was an even larger job.

I left New York with many thoughts about the resources we deploy, and how and if I should work to change the system. While our mission is to recover live humans, in New York and Oklahoma only the dead had been recovered. In defense of the system, it is designed to deal with earthquakes not terrorist incidents. There is a big difference in what happens to the site when the active mechanism is an explosive. In an explosion, many victims are killed outright. And more are killed by the shock wave that follows, even if they are found in what is normally thought of to be a "survivable" void where they are not crushed by debris. In an earthquake, victims in such voids are more likely to be found alive.

It is currently being debated whether it is better to cross-train live find dogs to also indicate deceased victims, to keep live find dogs and add cadaver dogs, or to have some of each on the Task Forces. There are many handlers who are encouraging the idea of cross-training the dogs. Some dogs and handlers could do this successfully, however not all dogs can be cross-trained and not all handlers have the expertise needed to cross-train the dog. I think it is an extremely dangerous option. My concern on this issue is that a dog may get confused and frustrated and give the wrong alert on a dead person and cause a live person to possibly die by concentrating resources in a low priority area. The rationale that all we find are dead victims and therefore it really doesn't make a lot of difference, is unacceptable to me. I believe that a dog that has a single purpose is the best resource. It is my opinion that the Task Force should have both live find specialists and human remains specialists.

To each incident that FEMA and the various Task Forces respond, new issues will arise and changes to the current system will have to be implemented. By studying the effectiveness and efficiency of the system for each incident that occurs, disaster response efforts will continue to evolve in a positive direction.

APPENDIX A

CANINE FITNESS

Many handlers overlook the physical conditioning aspect of training their dogs. This should be viewed as a crucial part of your training program. If you want to get the best performance possible from your Disaster Search Dog, you need to keep the dog in peak performance shape. The dog's exercise program should include endurance, strength, cardiovascular fitness, and coordination drills. Remember, with any exercise program, your dog must be in sound health in the first place. The dog needs to be at a good working weight; a fat dog cannot perform well. If your dog is overweight, you may need to start slowly with the amount and type of exercises and gradually increase the difficulty of the program as the dog gains strength. Don't forget to consider the dog's diet and make adjustments if needed.

ENDURANCE

Building endurance is the key to a good fitness program for the canine athlete. The program you adopt to build endurance needs to be fun and it should be something that the handler and dog can do together. A few exercises like hiking, jogging, swimming, or bike riding will benefit the handler as well. If you choose bike riding, a good goal for a DSD would include a three to six mile bike ride two to three times a week.

With any kind of endurance road work physical stress is placed on the leg bones, joints, and pads. The dog should be worked on dirt or grass for the major part of the workout program. Asphalt and concrete will wear out the dog's pads very quickly, and this kind of injury will take weeks to heal. The dog's pads should be checked on a regular basis during this type of training.

Weather and temperature are both important factors to consider when exercising your dog. Most people are very conscious about the possibility of over heating (hyperthermia) and the danger that it presents to the dog. But there are also dangers in very cold climates as well. Wind velocity and direction are important factors that can affect your dog's body temperature. Running for extended periods of time into the wind may cause a fatigued dog to become chilled, especially for dogs that are not acclimated to a cold climate. Because the dog's mouth is responsible for cooling the body, drawing in large quantities of frigid air may cause the dog's core temperature to drop (hypothermia) to a dangerous low. Swimming is one of the best exercises for building endurance. It is a low-impact activity that can increase endurance and strength and is an especially good exercise for the hotter months where heat exhaustion is an issue. Your dog may need to wear a canine life vest if he is new to swimming or if you plan on swimming your dog for long durations of time. It is recommended that you start a swimming program slowly, increasing the distance as he is physically able. Additionally, you may want to have a collar and leash on the dog, just in case you need to assist the dog to exit the water if he becomes too tired or panicked.

Francis Metcalf, a noted expert in canine fitness, recommends a well rounded training routine. He stresses that in order to maintain optimal health and weight that three categories of exercise are essential, including endurance, strength, and coordination training. He suggests taking a long walk with the dog to warm up first. This is also a good time to observe your dog for possible injuries or lameness before starting on the exercise program for the day.

FITNESS GAMES

Two Hose Game

While bicycling is a great exercise to build endurance, wind sprints can be beneficial for cardiovascular fitness and variety. The following exercise/game is described in the book *Schutzhund Obedience, Training in Drive* by Gottfried Dildei and Sheila Booth.

This game is played on a grass field and the object is for the dog to chase a hose, toy, ball or bumper, retrieve it, and as the dog approaches the handler, the handler commands the dog to "drop it." As the dog drops the bumper, the handler throws *another* bumper in the direction the dog is traveling. So, the dog races up and down the field chasing, retrieving, and dropping the bumper near you as he races after the one you have just thrown. This is an excellent game for dogs that have a strong prey/play drive. Throw the bumper until the dog no longer runs after it or lies down. Watch the dog carefully for signs of exhaustion. The number of repetitions should be built up slowly. It is important to observe how the dog turns as it picks up the bumper. If the dog tends to pivot on the front leg as it picks up the bumper while in motion, this may not be a good exercise for the dog to perform because he may develop "tennis elbow," causing pain and possible damage. If the dog slows first to pick up the bumper and then turns wide, this would be a safe exercise for your dog. This drill is an excellent way for a dog to release stress, as well as improve physical fitness.

Weight Pulling

Athletes pump iron to build strength and muscle mass. Weight pulling improves cardiovascular capacity, builds muscle mass, and strength. There are several options for your dog to participate in this kind of activity. You may want to invest in a weight pulling harness that is suitable for pulling, sledding, or skijoring. Commercial sleds can be purchased or you can use old vehicle tires.

First, the dog must learn that it is all right for something to drag behind him. In order to get the dog moving forward while pulling something, have a 6-foot leash on the dog, step in front of the dog, and offer a treat as you coach the dog to heel with you. The dog gets a treat and learns that the weight behind will not run over or hurt it. *It is best to start the dog pulling light loads over short distances.* Once the dog has learned to pull forward, the handler should slowly increase the distance the dog must pull the weight and then, slowly increase the weight load. Do not increase both dimensions at the same time.

Backstop Fetch

This game is a combination of endurance and coordination. The game is to throw the ball (approximately 50 feet) against a backstop. The dog races to the backstop to catch it as it bounces off the backstop or to field a ground ball. A good retriever will complete anywhere from 30-100 repetitions in cool weather. Be sure to keep the ball height low so that the dog will not have to jump in the air to catch it. Otherwise, this could lead to potential back injuries.

The Flirt Pole

This game is similar to a popular cat game, in which a string is tied to a long pole with a target (cloth, catnip, feather toy) at the other end of the string. The flirt pole for dogs needs to be constructed of materials that are more substantial than the cat toy—no surprise there! The target can be a tennis ball, sock, or rag, but needs to be lightweight enough so that it can be whipped around quickly. The object is to make the dog spin and weave while trying to catch the target. Some dogs learn to watch and try to predict the direction of travel and catch the prey. The dog must be allowed to catch the target every now and then. This is the dog's reward for a good chase. It is the handler's job to keep the game unpredictable and exciting.

Barrel Rolling

This is a wonderful game to teach coordination skills, although it may take a little time for the dog to learn how to balance and move the barrel or spool. The large wooden spools used to hold heavy electric wire will work very well for the initial lessons. The larger the diameter of the spool, the easier it is for the dog to control. Teach the dog to "hup up" onto the spool spindle and to balance himself on it. Stand in front of the spool or use blocks to limit movement of the spool until the dog learns to keep his balance on his own. Once the dog can balance on the spool, slowly roll the spool away from you (backwards). This forces the dog to walk forward. Do this exercise on grass first, which will help control how the barrel rolls, until the dog is skilled enough and can roll the barrel in either direction. Once the dog is skilled at the large spool, you can increase the difficulty of the exercise by decreasing the diameter of the spool diameter, which makes the spool more sensitive to the dog's movement. The value of barrel rolling, besides being a neat parlor trick, is that it requires intense balancing ability in a controlled setting. The dog learns to make quick adjustments in his center of gravity. Barrel rolling is an excellent exercise for dogs involved in disaster searching.

Uphill Stick Jumping

Jumping uphill decreases the impact on the front quarters of the dog. The additional strength required to jump uphill, combined with less foreleg strain, makes this a good agility/strength exercise. Start the exercise on a gentle hill, placing the dog a good distance away from you. Move uphill of your dog with the jump stick held low for an easy jump. The dog will quickly learn that it needs more momentum (power) to jump uphill. As the dog's strength and skill increase, you can move the dog closer to the jump stick for better form. To increase the difficulty of the exercise, use steeper and steeper hills and slightly raise the jump stick.

Pull Uphill and Heel Downhill

This is a good exercise for warming up or for a dog that needs gentle conditioning due to injury or age. Any area with a variety of rolling hills will be acceptable for the training location. Fit the dog with a pulling harness, tracking harness, or walking harness, a training collar, and a six-foot leash. Throw your dog's favorite toy up to the crest of the hill. Encourage the dog to pull you up the hill to get his toy. Let the dog enjoy it for a brief moment and then pick up the toy. Use the toy to keep the dog's focus on your face as you heel down the hill. To maximize the workout, have the dog pull you very slowly up the hill. This will increase the amount of time the muscles stay contracted. As you slowly go down hill, reward the dog for maintaining himself in heel position. This is a great training technique for dogs that forge ahead of their handlers. Once the dog is comfortable with the exercise, increase the difficulty by finding steeper hills, sand, or gravel hills.

APPENDIX B

SCENT AND SCENT PATTERNS

WHAT IS SCENT?

Scent can be defined as an odor that a live, dead, or inanimate object emits. Everything in the world has its own distinct odor. Every object is composed of active molecules and particles. Scent can be readily accessible or barely accessible according to the thermal energy of the particles which cause the scent to become airborne. Some objects shed their surface particles more easily than others. This process may include bacterial degradation and rejuvenation processes, such as in the shedding of old dead skin.

It is common knowledge that the physiology of the canine olfactory system is unique and different from that of humans. The canine nose has the ability to detect a wide spectrum of odors or scents. Dogs have 220 million receptor sites in their noses whereas humans only have around 5 million receptors. Dogs form scent pictures about their environment while humans form visual pictures. The dog has the unique ability to discriminate scent, detecting a faint odor system within very a strong odor system. The human nose cannot do this. The strong odor system will mask or cover the faint odor so that a human can't detect it. There are many good books and articles written about the physiology of the canine nose and olfactory system, such as *Scent: Training to Track, Search, and Rescue*, by Milo Pearsall and Hugo Verbruggen, M.D. This book contains an excellent section on the physiology of the canine nose and olfactory system and includes some good information about scent.

The living body is a scent source that continually renews itself and is always generating scent. Chemical changes taking place on the surface of the body speed up the molecular exchange with the surrounding air currents and release the scent particles of lighter mass into the surrounding air, thereby forming the scent plume (scent cone) for which air scenting dogs are searching. The heavier particles fall to the ground as the body moves and are available for the tracking dog to utilize for a period of time. The trailing dog uses a combination of the lighter weight particles deposited on brush, rocks, and around depressions, as well as the heavier particles that lodge in crevices or areas protected from the elements. All of these particles of scent are susceptible to degradation from time, heat, moisture, and bacterial action.

HOW WEATHER AND TEMPERATURE IMPACT SCENT PATTERNS

The handler must be aware of all of the factors that influence a scent pattern, such as topography, wind, temperature, humidity, and atmospheric conditions, in order to successfully read and manage the dog. The dog's nose is unique, but it should not be the only resource being used. The handler is part of the team and his knowledge is important to effectively deploy the dog.

Temperature varies considerably, in both time and space and for various reasons, most of which is caused by the heating or cooling of the earth's surface. The difference in temperatures creates variations in air density and atmospheric pressure and, therefore, causes vertical and horizontal air movement. There is a lot to learn about air movement that is beyond the scope of this book. To learn more about weather and temperature factors I recommend reading *Fire Weather: Agriculture Handbook 360* from the US Department of Agriculture's Forest Service. It can be ordered through *Search Gear* at 1-800-474-2612 or www.search-gear.com.

Here are some of the very basic concepts and terminology describing air movement and topography of which you should be aware.

Slope winds are local winds present on all sloping surfaces. The air movement will be up slope during the early part of the day as a result of surface heating. Slope winds are present in disaster sites where there are large slabs at an angle or partially collapsed walls that are leaning. The reverse happens at night, in that cool air travels down slope following the path of least resistance, much like water flowing down hill. This transition starts to happen in the late afternoon as the area falls into shadow and the surface begins to cool.

Valley winds are winds that blow up-valley by day and down-valley by night. The small mountain valleys and canyons are heated quickly during the day and cool quickly at night due to the smaller ratio of air volume in the valley to the greater volume of land mass. As the valley winds increase in speed, they influence the upslope winds causing them to move up-valley. This concept can apply to some disaster scenes as well. In very large disaster sites, such as the World Trade Center in New York, collapsed buildings created some very deep valleys. While these valleys are not as large as natural valleys found in the wilderness, they generate interesting scent problems of which the handler should be aware.

Eddy formation is a common characteristic in uneven terrain and applies to disaster rubble as well. Eddies are defined as turbulent air forces formed when air flows over or around an obstacle. A huge boulder or rock outcropping or a partially collapsed wall may cause an eddy on the upwind side. This turbulent air swirls around and creates difficult areas for the dog to search. It is necessary for the dog to search these areas carefully. *A general rule of thumb is that the area of the eddy will be 8-10 times the height of the obstacle causing the eddy*. This gives the handler a rough idea of how large an area must be fine-searched. High bluffs, canyon rims, and the wall of tall buildings will most likely have upslope currents in the morning and large rolling eddies on the lee side. There may also be a dead air space right at the foot of the tall building.

Chimney effect occurs during midday when the sun heats the air causing the scent to rise straight up. This can happen in open rubble piles when the temperature is high and there is no perceivable air movement. The chimney effect can be very confusing to the dogs. The dog must do a fine search in order to detect the scent rising straight up in the air. Chimney effects occur most frequently when the sun is right overhead at midday. Searching during this time of day is the least productive in high temperatures and requires the dog to do fine searches for short periods of time, take frequent rest breaks, and drink lots of water to prevent dehydration.

Laminar flow refers to air that moves along in layers, is very consistent, and very stable. It is more likely to occur at night, which is why night searches with dogs are very effective in rubble fields.

Scent pools can best be described as a collection of scent particles, usually the result of scent flowing downhill and being dammed up by a barrier. This obstruction causes a large collection of particles to be deposited in a somewhat confined area, like a small bowl or depression in the rubble. The scent source may be uphill or may be somewhere inside the scent pool. The scent pool is continually being supplied with scent particles, making it difficult for some dogs to pinpoint the location of the source. Once the handler realizes the dog is in a scent pool, it may be necessary for him to assist the dog in a fine search, using the wind direction and terrain features to help locate the victim according to how the scent pool is being formed.

All of the conditions discussed above will affect how the handler should plan an efficient search strategy. Learning as much as possible about how scent travels will help dog handlers to manage their dogs in an efficient manner. Whenever possible, it is the handler's responsibility to direct the dog to search areas so that the dog can take advantage of the best scenting conditions. Some very prophetic person said, "The dog can only find what it can scent and the dog can only scent the subject if he is upwind from a subject."

APPENDIX C
PUPPY AND YOUNG ADULT DOG EVALUATION

Puppy testing for potential Disaster Search Dogs should begin at around 49 days of age. The testing should be conducted in an area of the house that is not familiar to the puppies. The following are my comments on evaluating the puppies using the *modified* Puppy Aptitude Test guidelines developed by Wendy Volhard in her book *The Puppy Personality Profile*. The first three tests should be done with all of the puppies together.

Test #1: Stranger Approach
A stranger approaches the puppies in a normal manner, without speaking. The evaluator will observe and note the puppies' reactions. Then the evaluator will talk happily to the puppies and note the puppies' reactions. Is the puppy happy, friendly, and confident? That is the desired reaction for a search dog.

Test #2: Recovery Attitude
The evaluator tosses a large plastic bottle into the pen so that it lands about 10 ft away from the puppies. Observe the puppies for five minutes. This is testing the surprise element and reaction to a strange object. The degree of the startle response and recovery time is very important. Almost all puppies will startle, but how quickly they recover and investigate the foreign object is the most important behavior. The puppy should notice, investigate with confidence, and even try to bite or carry the bottle. Some will paw or hit it with their front feet. This is good. Some may investigate confidently, but bark at it instead of touching it. This behavior is all right for a search dog. Which puppies are the leaders? If the puppies have been exposed to plastic bottles, try another startle test by dropping a large book or metal pot on the floor.

Test #3: Possessiveness Among Littermates
Have the breeder toss a meat bone into the pen and note the puppies' reactions for five minutes. This is where you may see a big difference in the puppies. See

which puppy grabs the bone and fends off all other puppies or grabs the bones and runs to keep possession. The puppy that fights to keep possession is going to be a very dominant dog that will need firm handling. The puppy that grabs the bone and runs is probably the better choice, although the puppy that grabs it and gives it up to the more dominant dog is also a reasonable choice.

I once observed a litter being tested and three puppies had to be separated to stop the fighting over the bone. Several other littermates were partly engaged in the fight and barking on the edge. Puppies exhibiting this barking behavior (a more normal behavior) may be a possible choice for a search dog over the "fighters."

The remainder of the test is done with one puppy at a time in another area that is not familiar to the puppy. This area must be out of sight, hearing, and scent of the other puppies, the mother, and the owner of the litter.

Test #4: Reaction to a Strange Area

The evaluator places the puppy on the floor/grass in the middle of the test area. Quickly stand back and observe the pup. Do not touch or speak for two to three minutes. The puppies that investigate with confidence or even caution are the more confident puppies and are good candidates for search dogs. These pups are demonstrating some independence and curiosity.

Test #5: Pup's Willingness to Go To/ Bond with a New Person

The evaluator places the puppy in the middle of the test area, kneels down, and gently claps hands while calling to attract the puppy. The willingness to approach people is a very important behavior. A search dog needs to be confident. So, a puppy that investigates with confidence or caution is a good choice. Investigation is the most important behavior to me. We have already seen the group reaction to a stranger and now we want to see how the puppy will react on its own when invited to come and visit. The dog that comes quickly with tail up and engages the new person by jumping on them, licking, and even nipping or tugging on clothing is a good choice. The puppy that came with tail down and didn't engage the new person is more questionable. It is possible that this dog, through proper socialization, can increase its level of confidence, but this is probably not a good candidate.

Test #6: Following Response

The evaluator places the puppy in the middle of the test area making sure that the puppy sees her walk away in a normal manner. Acceptable behaviors for a puppy to exhibit include quickly following behind the evaluator with tail up, getting under foot, and nibbling or tugging on clothing. The degree of confidence may be related to the amount of interaction with the evaluator. However, all of these behaviors are acceptable responses and indicate which puppies are reasonable choices for a search dog prospect.

Test #7: Response to Affection
The evaluator stands the pup on all four feet and gently strokes along the pup's back from head to tail for 30 seconds or until a clear behavior reaction happens. The puppy that will not accept affection/attention from the evaluator for 30 seconds without biting and growling is not a good candidate. The puppy that jumps up and paws or stands until you stop the petting is more manageable and will be a better choice.

Test #8: Pup's Reaction to Dominance
The evaluator places the puppy on its back on the floor and holds him there with a hand on the puppy's chest. Hold the puppy in this position for 20 to 30 seconds. If the puppy becomes aggressive and tries to bite, he is not a good choice. The better choice is the pup that struggles, accepts and relaxes, or the pup that is unconcerned and relaxed.

Test #9: Response to Lifting
The evaluator holds the pup securely in both hands and lifts him up and away from the body. Hold the pup in this extended position for 20 seconds. If the pup becomes aggressive and tries to bite, he is not a good choice. The pup that struggles and then relaxes is a better choice.

Test #10: Curiosity
The evaluator shakes a soda can with pennies inside it to make noise. This tests the pup for sound sensitivity, as well as curiosity. Observe the pup's response to the noise and then lightly toss the can a few feet in front of the pup. The puppy should either notice the noise and investigate it with confidence or show no concern after noticing the noise. Some puppies will startle and this is normal. However, the startle response should only last a few seconds and then the puppy should show some interest in the object. Curiosity is a good response.

Test #11: Retrieve Instinct
The evaluator uses a ball, paper ball, or soft toy to slightly tease the pup and then gently roll it on the ground or floor in front of the puppy. Next, she should gently roll the object away from the puppy and observe the response. The puppy

that chases and retrieves or chases and runs away with the toy is the best choice. The puppy that chases but does not pick up the object is demonstrating prey drive, an important drive, making this puppy a possible candidate as well.

Test #12: Tug-of-War

This game is played with a sock or small rolled towel. The evaluator waves the sock back and forth in front of the puppy to start the game and then pulls it along the floor in a jerking motion. If the puppy bites, holds on, or shakes it, the evaluator should let the puppy pull it from her hand. The puppy that grabs the sock then tugs, shakes, and carries it off, or the puppy that grabs the sock and tugs, shakes, but drops it when no pressure is exerted are all good choices. The puppy that grabs the sock and tugs without shaking is also a possibility.

Test #13: Scenting Ability

In a new, nearby location, have the evaluator drag a fresh bone on the grass/ ground for 15-20 feet or lay a food-baited track with cheese for the same distance. Release the puppy at the start of the track. The puppy should be getting hungry, so he should search for food. The puppy that follows the track using his nose or the puppy that is excited and searches using both its nose and eyes are good choices. If a puppy runs around looking and does not try to scent or hunt for the food, he is not a good choice. Remember, the hunt drive is very important. This test gives you some information about the dog's scenting ability and hunt drive.

Test #14: Possessiveness with Humans

The evaluator gives the puppy a bone to chew on for 2-3 minutes. Next, she approaches the puppy and attempts to take the bone away. If the puppy guards, threatens, or tries to bite the evaluator, this puppy is not a good choice. If the puppy growls and grabs the bone and runs away, the puppy should still be considered, though this is not the best response. The puppy that grabs and runs away with the bone is a better choice.

Before continuing the test, it is time to take a break. Let the pups play, relax or nap. Then start the testing again in about 15-20 minutes.

Test #15: Touch Sensitivity

This test gives the evaluator some idea of the puppy's pain tolerance. This is accomplished by squeezing the webbing between two toes on a front paw. The evaluator squeezes the webbing between a finger and the thumb lightly, and then increases the pressure while counting to ten. Stop pressing as soon as the pup pulls away or shows discomfort. The puppy is graded on the number count prior to showing discomfort. A higher number count signifies a higher tolerance to pain. Puppies with middle to high tolerance for pain are preferred.

Test #16: Sound Sensitivity

The evaluator places the puppy in the center of the test area. The evaluator or assistant makes a sharp, clattering noise a few feet away by placing one or two large spoons in a metal pan, rattling it, and then dropping the pan on the floor four to five feet away from the puppy. The puppy should turn toward the noise, listen, and locate it. Watch for the puppy that shows curiosity and approaches the pan. If the puppy barks and touches the object, this puppy is very self-confident and may be difficult to manage. The puppy that listens, locates, shows curiosity, and walks toward the pan, or locates the sound, barks, and circles the pan, but doesn't touch it, is a good choice.

EVALUATION PROCESS FOR YOUNG ADULT DOGS

This evaluation process includes testing the dog for aggression toward humans and other dogs, assessing the hunt drive, prey/play drive, and the ability to negotiate unpleasant, complex surfaces, and sound sensitivity. The test should be performed in a neutral training area that can accommodate the physical needs of the test, as well as the noisy machinery.

The testing process begins using the Federal Emergency Management Agency (FEMA) National Canine Readiness Evaluation criteria, Type II aggression testing process. The dog must demonstrate he/she is friendly or accepting of strange humans and dogs. The dog must be at least 12 months of age. There is an excellent screening/evaluation tool for assessing a disaster search dog on the Internet at http://www.disasterdog.org/forms.htm.

Test #1: Canine Is Not Aggressive To Humans

The handler ties the dog to a fence and then leaves him unattended without any obedience commands. The handler proceeds to a designated area out of the dog's sight. After one minute, a stranger approaches the dog in a calm, non-threatening manner, unties the dog, and returns the dog to the handler. The dog should not demonstrate fear, stress, or aggression to the stranger.

Test #2: Canine Is Not Aggressive To Other Canines

The AKC Figure 8 obedience exercise is used to test any canine aggression towards other dogs. The testing dog must be capable of completing a Figure 8 around two handlers with their dogs (post teams) on lead, sitting at their side, and spaced eight feet apart. The testing team shall complete the pattern with a loose lead, passing within two feet of each of the post teams. The dog should not show any aggressive behavior toward either of the post teams.

Test #3: Assessing Hunt Drive

The handler walks the dog on lead and in the heel position to an area of tall weeds and some brush. The handler takes the dog off lead and tosses the dog's favorite toy into the brush or tall weeds while the dog sits at the heel position watching. The dog watches the handler toss the toy and sees where the toy has landed. The dog is released to find it and should search for and find the toy within 2-3 minutes. If the dog is not successful in finding the toy, determine whether he was distracted and repeat this exercise in another area. A dog who is unable to find the toy on the second try is not demonstrating that he has the hunt drive needed for search work and this may be a cause for concern.

The next step is to have a helper toss the toy deeper into thicker brush. The dog is sitting in the heel position with his/her back towards the target area. The dog *does not* see where the toy is tossed or where it has landed. The dog is then released to go find the toy. If the dog is not successful on this exercise, he is demonstrating a lack of hunt drive and is not a good candidate for a Disaster Search Dog.

The final step is to toss the toy deep into the brush area and then heel the dog away from the area. Bring the dog back after one minute and release the dog to find the toy. This procedure demonstrates the dog's hunt drive, which is necessary for a DSD. They have to be able to continue to search in unpleasant, complex areas, often over long periods of time.

Test #4: Assessing Dog's Play/Prey Drive

This is accomplished by having the handler play with the dog off-lead using the dog's favorite play toy. This demonstrates the handler's relationship with the dog and the willingness of the canine to engage in play or to choose his own agenda. The next step is to see if the dog will play with another handler/trainer who is friendly and experienced in motivating dogs.

Some dogs do not like to play games. A few of these dogs that do not like to play will work well with a food reward system. The handler/trainer can put some hotdogs in a sock and tease the dog like you would play with a cat. Keep the food away from the dog and see if the dog remains focused on getting the food. If the dog is food-oriented he will engage in a game to get the food. If the dog is not interested in the handler/trainer for the food reward, then there is a problem. The lack of a play/prey or food reward drive does raise a red flag. The play/prey or food drive is an essential element in developing a reward system. If the dog is not interested in playing, doesn't seem to have much prey drive, and is not food oriented, he is not a good candidate as a working dog.

Test #5: Assessing Sound Sensitivity

The handler, with the dog on lead, begins a simple obedience heeling exercise. The heeling pattern should take the dog close to some noise-making machinery. Once the dog is performing the heeling pattern, start the machinery, leaf blower, chain saw, or pneumatic nailer. Next, have a person pound on a sheet metal building as you heel the dog by it. Watch for any behavior changes and continue heeling the dog into the building if the dog seems comfortable. It is not uncommon for a dog to startle if some machinery is turned on unexpectedly as he passes. It is important to assess how quickly the dog recovers from being startled and whether he is able to focus on the handler and the heeling exercise. A dog that does not recover quickly and is stressed by the exercise is not a good candidate for the job.

Appendix D
FEMA Building Markings and Construction Plans for Training Equipment

FEMA US&R BUILDING MARKING SYSTEM
MAIN ENTRANCE SEARCH MARKING

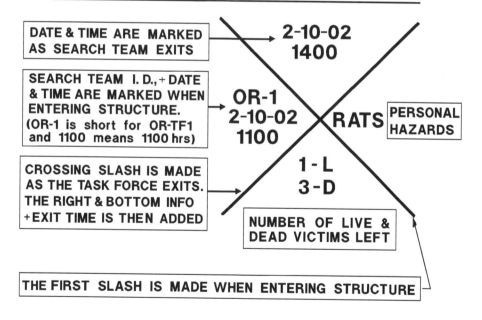

DATE & TIME ARE MARKED AS SEARCH TEAM EXITS → 2-10-02 1400

SEARCH TEAM I. D., + DATE & TIME ARE MARKED WHEN ENTERING STRUCTURE. (OR-1 is short for OR-TF1 and 1100 means 1100 hrs) → OR-1 2-10-02 1100

RATS

PERSONAL HAZARDS

CROSSING SLASH IS MADE AS THE TASK FORCE EXITS. THE RIGHT & BOTTOM INFO + EXIT TIME IS THEN ADDED → 1 - L 3 - D

NUMBER OF LIVE & DEAD VICTIMS LEFT

THE FIRST SLASH IS MADE WHEN ENTERING STRUCTURE

TASK FORCE BUILDING MARKING SYSTEM
STRUCTURE/HAZARDS EVALUATION

STRUCTURAL SPECIALIST MAKES A 2'x2' BOX ON BUILDING ADJACENT TO
MOST ACCESSIBLE ENTRY. THIS IS DONE AFTER DOING HAZARDS
ASSESSMENT AND FILLING OUT HAZARDS ASSESSMENT FORM. BOX IS
SPRAY PAINTED WITH INTL ORANGE AND MARKED AS FOLLOWS:

 STRUCTURE IS RELATIVELY SAFE FOR S&R OPERATIONS
DAMAGE IS SUCH THAT THERE IS LITTLE DANGER OF
FURTHER COLLAPSE.

 STRUCTURE IS SIGNIFICANTLY DAMAGED. SOME AREAS
MAY BE RELATIVELY SAFE, BUT OTHER AREAS MAY
NEED SHORING, BRACING, OR REMOVAL OF HAZARDS.
(MAY BE PANCAKED BLDG)

 STRUCTURE IS NOT SAFE FOR RESCUE OPERATIONS
AND MAY BE SUBJECT TO SUDDEN COLLAPSE. REMOTE
SEARCH OPERATIONS MAY PROCEED AT SIGNIFICANT RISK.
IF RESCUE OPERATIONS ARE UNDERTAKEN, SAFE HAVEN
AREAS & RAPID EVACUATION ROUTES SHOULD BE CREATED.

 ARROW LOCATED NEXT TO THE MARKING BOX INDICATES
THE DIRECTION OF SAFEST ENTRY TO THE STRUCTURE.

 INDICATES HAZMAT CONDITION IN OR ADJACENT TO
STRUCTURE. S&R OPERATIONS NORMALLY WILL NOT
BE ALLOWED UNTIL CONDITION IS BETTER DEFINED
OR ELIMINATED.

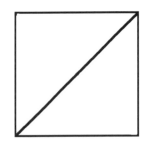 **15JUL92   1310 HRS**
HM - NATURAL GAS
OR-1

(DO NOT ENTER BUILDING
UNTIL GAS IS TURNED OFF)

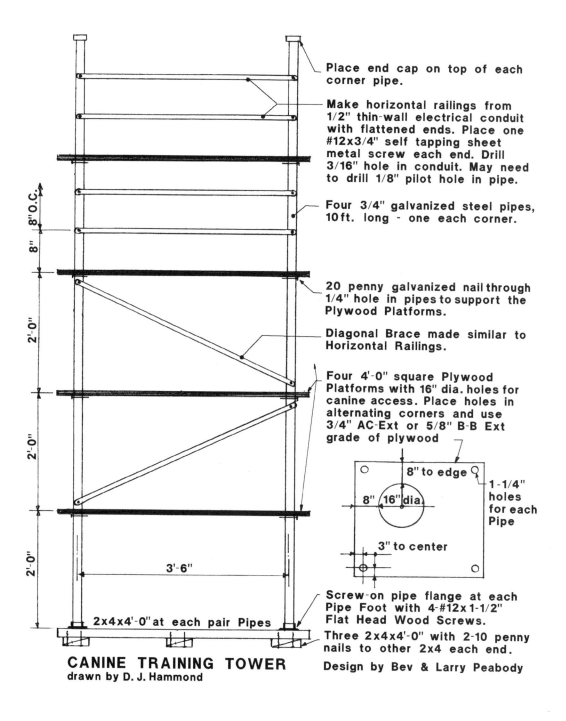

Place end cap on top of each corner pipe.

Make horizontal railings from 1/2" thin-wall electrical conduit with flattened ends. Place one #12x3/4" self tapping sheet metal screw each end. Drill 3/16" hole in conduit. May need to drill 1/8" pilot hole in pipe.

Four 3/4" galvanized steel pipes, 10 ft. long - one each corner.

20 penny galvanized nail through 1/4" hole in pipes to support the Plywood Platforms.

Diagonal Brace made similar to Horizontal Railings.

Four 4'-0" square Plywood Platforms with 16" dia. holes for canine access. Place holes in alternating corners and use 3/4" AC-Ext or 5/8" B-B Ext grade of plywood

8" to edge

1-1/4" holes for each Pipe

8" 16" dia.

3" to center

Screw-on pipe flange at each Pipe Foot with 4-#12x1-1/2" Flat Head Wood Screws.

Three 2x4x4'-0" with 2-10 penny nails to other 2x4 each end.

8" O.C.

8"

2'-0"

2'-0"

2'-0"

3'-6"

2x4x4'-0" at each pair Pipes

CANINE TRAINING TOWER
drawn by D. J. Hammond

Design by Bev & Larry Peabody

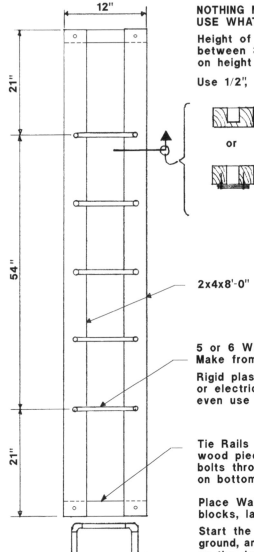

NOTHING NEEDS TO BE EXACT
USE WHATEVER YOU HAVE ON HAND

Height of Wickets should vary and be between 3" and 9" in height depending on height of smallest dog.

Use 1/2", 3/4" and/or 1" diameter pipe.

Drill holes to fit snug and leave about 3/8" at bottom.

or

Drill holes a little oversized and place a small piece of plywood under hole.

2x4x8'-0" or so for each Rail.

5 or 6 Wickets spaced a little unevenly. Make from 3 pieces of pipe and 2 elbows.

Rigid plastic pipe is easiest but steel pipe or electrical conduit will do. One can even use solid steel bent rods.

Tie Rails together at each end with 1x wood piece under Rails. Use 3/8" carriage bolts through Rails with nut and washer on bottom side.

Place Walk across two oil drums, wood blocks, ladders or whatever you have.

Start the training with Walk just above ground, and gradually increase the height as the dog becomes more comfortable.

Design by Bev & Larry Peabody

CANINE TRAINING WICKET WALK
drawn by D. J. Hammond

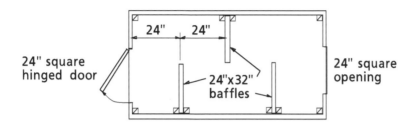

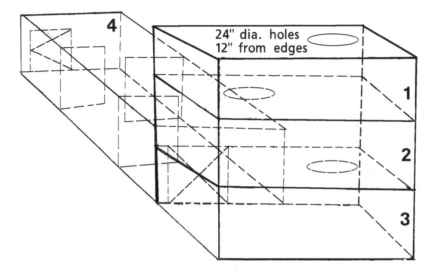

Four Boxes made from 3/4" plyw'd w/2x2 corner cleats thus:

Boxes 1 & 2 - 4'x8'x2' hi w/hole in top & no bottom.

Box 3 - 4'x8'x2' hi w/hole in top, solid bottom & 24" sq hole in side.

Box 4 - 4'x8'x2'-8" hi w/solid top & bott, 3- baffles, hinged door & 24"sq opng.

Use #8x2" Deck-Mate, phillips head coated screws @ 6"o.c. to fasten plyw'd at all edges.

Use Exterior Grade plyw'd and paint to reduce sun/rain damage.

METRO - CANINE TRAINING BAFFLE BOX
drawn by D. J. Hammond

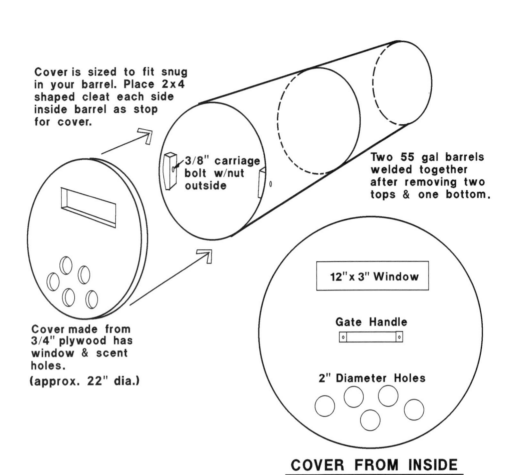

Cover is sized to fit snug in your barrel. Place 2x4 shaped cleat each side inside barrel as stop for cover.

3/8" carriage bolt w/nut outside

Two 55 gal barrels welded together after removing two tops & one bottom.

Cover made from 3/4" plywood has window & scent holes.
(approx. 22" dia.)

12"x 3" Window

Gate Handle

2" Diameter Holes

COVER FROM INSIDE

1. Window should be made of Plexi-glass. It will get scratched & broken The trim that is used to hold glass should be placed on three sides so that new piece can be slid in place without fuss.

2. Handle inside is very important. It should be strong and connected with thru bolts. Rope, wire on eye hooks, plumbers tape, etc. have been tried and eventually break.

ALERT BARREL with WOOD COVER
drawn by D. J. Hammond

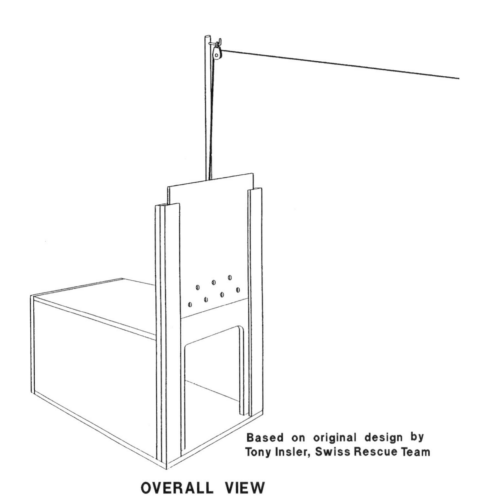

Based on original design by
Tony Insler, Swiss Rescue Team

OVERALL VIEW

BARK TRAINING BOX with REMOTE OPENING DOOR
drawn by D. J. Hammond

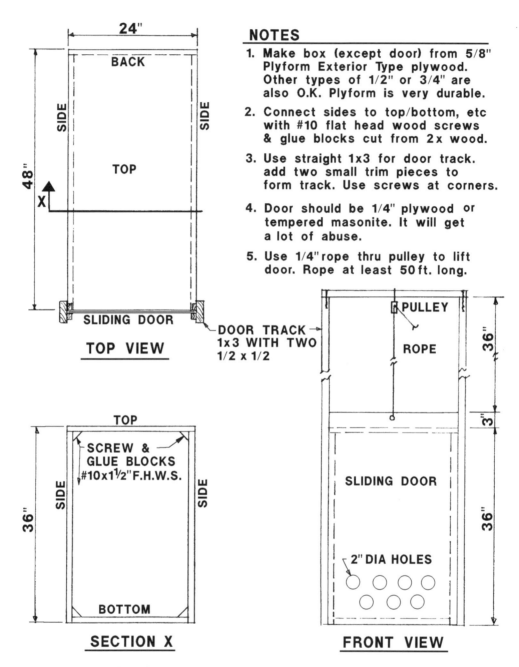

NOTES

1. Make box (except door) from 5/8"
   Plyform Exterior Type plywood.
   Other types of 1/2" or 3/4" are
   also O.K. Plyform is very durable.

2. Connect sides to top/bottom, etc
   with #10 flat head wood screws
   & glue blocks cut from 2x wood.

3. Use straight 1x3 for door track.
   add two small trim pieces to
   form track. Use screws at corners.

4. Door should be 1/4" plywood or
   tempered masonite. It will get
   a lot of abuse.

5. Use 1/4" rope thru pulley to lift
   door. Rope at least 50 ft. long.

BARK TRAINING BOX with REMOTE OPENING DOOR
drawn by D. J. Hammond

APPENDIX E
INTERVIEW CHECKLIST

The interview checklist or "Cheat Sheet" was designed to help handlers remember important questions to ask about the search incident and to gather important information needed to search the area and establish scene safety.

Time of collapse? _____

Type of occupancy? _____

Known missing? _____

Suspected missing? _____

Searched before? _____

Structural engineering check? _____

Findings? _____

Safe entry? _____

Prints? _____

Hazmat Checked? _____

Findings? _____

Utilities (who and how secured)? _____

Gas? _____

Electricity? _____

Water? _____

Rescue available? _____

Medical? _____

Vet? _____

APPENDIX F

GLOSSARY OF KEY TERMS

acclimate: Become accustomed to a different environment.

Air Scent Dog & Wilderness Search Dog: Common terms for Search & Rescue dogs with the ability and training to detect live human airborne scent particles, carried by air currents that lead the dog to find a lost person.

alert: A trained response when the dog has located the scent source or object it has been imprinted to find.

back chain: The process in which the training starts with teaching the end behavior first and then training all the small steps that lead up to that end behavior and linking them all together.

bait: Refers to food or the process of using food to encourage the canine to perform a behavior. Another name for food reward.

bark alert: The dog remains at the scent source and barks until the handler comes and give the dog another command.

blind search: Neither the handler or the dog knows where the victim is located.

BO: Base of Operations is the forward workstation at the rescue site near the assignment.

chain together: Training a series of small behaviors and then linking them together to make a more complex behavior.

clicker: A noisemaker or toy that clicks and is used to mark a specific behavior that is being shaped the instant the behavior is performed.

CSS: Canine Search Specialist, the dog handler.

dog team: One dog and the handler.

DHS: Department of Homeland Security.

false alert: The dog alerts for no apparent reason or improperly alerts on a non human scent source.

FEMA: The Federal Emergency Management Agency.

fine search: A directed search where the search grids are close together.

fixed schedule: The same repetitive schedule; every third time the dog is rewarded.

free search: The dog is free to search without any direction from the handler.

foundation: Fundamental, basic and essential skills, the basis of anything considered as the support for the future structure.

generalize: The dog has learned the behavior and can perform the behavior in other environments. Dogs that have learned a behavior at home need to be able to perform that behavior in other environments.

grid search: A controlled methodical search using a grid or defined pattern to ensure coverage of the area.

hasty search: A quick search of the area.

HS: Hazmat Specialist that monitor air quality and other gasses.

helper: A trainer or very experienced person that inter-acts with the dog during training.

indication: In some areas of the country the word indication is used to describe the trained (alert) behavior. The two words Alert and Indication refer to the same behavior.

lure: The process whereby the canine is baited or enticed with food to perform a behavior.

place learners: Dogs learn best when the training consists of short training sessions in the same place until the behavior is trained. Once the behavior is consistent the training must move to all different kinds of environments.

positive reinforcement: Adding something the dog likes causing the dog to want to repeat the behavior. Strengthening the behavior by presenting a desirable consequence.

proofing: The process of exposing the dog to different environments and distractions confirming the learned behavior.

reinforcer: Something that causes the behavior to be repeated like a food/toy reward.

reward: It may be food or a toy used to tell the dog he has done a good job. It should be something the dog is crazy about or will stand on his head to get.

reward system: A systematic way of rewarding the dog. The dog performs a behavior to get something from the handler (food/toy).

scent cone: Scent particles are blown on air currents in a cone shaped pattern, narrow at the origin and wider at the base. The velocity of the air currents determines the shape and length of the scent cone.

scent pool: A collection of scent particles in an area that may not be where the origin of the scent is located. The particles may be trapped in a corner of a building, in a depression or otherwise defined area.

shaping a behavior: A technique which involves rewarding the dog's best initial effort that approximates a desired behavior and then gradually raising the criteria until the desired behavior is formed.

STM: Search Team Manager.

target: An object that one aims at or an object that the handler directs the dog toward.

Task Force: The name attached to an organized unit consisting of about seventy people trained in disaster skills that is capable of responding to a disaster incident.

tracking: The dog follows the scented path that a human makes by walking or running and locates the human or articles touched by that human.

trailing dog: Used by law enforcement and search & rescue to find a human. The dog is trained to follow a specific scent that may not be exactly where the human walked but the scent particles are collected on depressions, rock and grass and brush along the way.

US&R System: Urban Search and Rescue System, refers to the organized response of trained responders to disaster incidents.

variable schedule: In canine use, it refers to how often the toy/ food reward is given. In a variable schedule the dog never knows when the reward will come. The dog may be rewarded after completing 2, 9, 7,15 or 27 behaviors.

SHIRLEY M. HAMMOND

Shirley has more than 28 years of Search and Rescue experiences. She has trained and certified dogs in area search, cadaver, disaster, evidence and water search. As a Training Advisor and Instructor for California Rescue Dog Association Inc. Shirley has mentored many teams through wilderness, cadaver, water and the FEMA Disaster Search Certification process. Among Shirley's most significant disaster search deployments are the Mexico City earthquake 1985, San Bernardino train wreck 1989, Loma Prieta earthquake 1989, Hurricane Iniki 1992, Oklahoma City bombing 1995 and the World Trade Center disaster 2001.

Currently, Shirley gives seminars on Disaster Search Dog training and Human Remains Detection. She lives in Palo Alto, California with her husband David and a red female Doberman who is certified as a Human Remains Detection Dog. David Hammond is deployed to FEMA disaster as a Structural Specialist and teaches classes for other Engineers and Rescue Personnel. His 45 years as a Structural Engineer make him well suited to these jobs. They have three grown children and three grandsons.

Shirley Hammond's current activities and background include:
- National and international instructor and evaluator for Human Remains Detection and Disaster Canine Evaluations and Training.
- Nationally rostered lead evaluator for testing FEMA Type I and Type II Disaster Dogs.
- Lead instructor for the California Office of Emergency Services OES/FEMA, Urban Search and Response (US&R) Canine Search Specialist Training Course.
- Member of the Board of Directors of the Santa Clara Medical Examiner-Coroner's Canine Specialized Search Team.
- Member of the Board of Directors for the Institute for Canine Forensics.
- A member and Canine Coordinator for California Task Force 3, based in Menlo Park, California.
- Evaluator for the California OES State Cadaver test, a member of the California OES/FEMA US&R System.
- Member of the NASA Disaster Assistance and Rescue Team.
- Member of the National Association for Search and Rescue.
- Past member of the California OES Canine Search Specialist Working Group.
- Past member of the FEMA Search Working Group Canine Subcommittee.
- Retired member of the California Rescue Dog Association.
- Involved in a research project using certified disaster dogs and wilderness dogs to determine live versus dead scent. Investigator for a Vegetation Study, Institute for Canine Forensics, to determine if plants absorb human remains scent particles and transpire those particles into the atmosphere.
- Shirley has retired a FEMA Type I certified dog Metrodobe's Spicey's Sunnyboy, "Sunny."